JUST DUST

An Improbable Marine's Vietnam Story

Just Dust - An improbable Marine's story. Copyright
©2015 by Wes Choc. All rights reserved.
Printed in the Unites States of America.
No part of this book shall be used or reproduced in any
manner whatsoever without written permission except
in the case of brief quotations embodied in critical
articles and reviews.

Chosen Journey Media books may be purchased for
educational, business or sales promotional use.
For information – www.weschoc.com

Library of Congress Cataloging in Publication Data
is available on request.

ISBN – 9780996389112 Second Edition.

Book management & marketing services
www.maxfemurmedia.com

Some of the most meaningful aspects of American 1960s culture were directly impacted by events in Vietnam. Some young men and women decided to play courageous roles on this historical stage . . . roles uniquely theirs to play and undeniably consequential . . . roles eliciting unusual encores for years to come.

These are several stories based upon my bit parts

Acknowledgements

To thank everyone who gave me encouragement to write *Just Dust* would be indeed a lengthy task. But in particular, I would like to acknowledge a few people in addition to my family whose assistance I very much value. To those who have listened to my stories, or who read my drafts, or who critiqued the ideas, I extend a special thanks: Jim Logan, Art and Janette Carr, Sue and Jim Opeka, Mike Davis, Riley Griffen, Jonathan Jackson, Thomas McArdle, and numerous others I've had coffee with. I thank them for listening, for asking astute questions, and for offering suggestions.

Facilitating the "how" part of publishing this book, I want to acknowledge the devotion of Tim Derrig who through personal suggestions, solid knowledge, and perpetual humor, was able to motivate me off dead center. A thank you here is insufficient recognition of this value.

Dedicated to my family and my friends . . .

First, I'd like to continue urging my children and grandchildren to read. There are so many stories to tell, and so many of these will never be written down. So, to our sons Brian, Jared, Tyler, and to grandchildren Parker, Adrienne, Keira, Camden, and Caspian, I urge you all to listen, to read, to grasp, to discuss, and yes, to write your own stories so others may enjoy your journeys in times yet to come.

Next, I want to recognize two Marine Corps friends who made a difference in my life, Steve White and Jim Logan. My rewards and journeys were possible because of them; they remain special to this day.

Most important, I want to dedicate these stories to the one who matters most, my wife, Carol Hoier Choc. For someone who had the courage to go to Vietnam herself (Red Cross), she knows more than most what treasures were sacrificed by so many.

And of course I don't want to overlook countless marines who surrendered life or limb …who sacrificed time and presence …who helped make a difference in so many other lives beyond their own.

Table of Contents

Acknowledgements vii
Dedication ix
Foreword xiii
Prologue... xv
Chapter 1 1
Chapter 2 11
Chapter 3 23
Chapter 4 31
Chapter 5 39
Chapter 6 59
Chapter 7 63
Chapter 8 71
Chapter 9 91
Chapter 10 93
Chapter 11 99
Chapter 12 107
Chapter 13 125
Chapter 14 137
Chapter 15 143
Chapter 16 157
Chapter 17 167
Chapter 18 175
Chapter 19 189
Chapter 20 201
Chapter 21 207

Foreword

If you met Wes Choc, the very last thing you would think: "That guy is a Marine!"

When I met Wes, he was an executive in a national organization …a thoughtful, pensive guy bringing much to the table, but who was often marginalized by his peers. Perhaps more philosopher than executive, Wes has a way of elevating conversations in search of truth and insight that wears down -- even annoys -- people less introspective. I found my own work with Wes both enlivening and exhausting. Wes is truly "curious" in both senses of the word: eagerly inquisitive and clearly eccentric.

It wasn't until many years later that I learned Wes is a Marine …and dumbfounded by the revelation! How could this awkward individual possibly fit into what may be the most standardized group of men in the world? Without doubt, Wes Choc is an improbable Marine.

Just Dust is also an improbable book. Part autobiographical narrative, part experiential thesis, Just Dust can be counted among the best soldiers' stories telling what happened to a man at war and in war. Equal parts external events and internal journey, the book is engaging, insightful, even downright funny.

Everyone knows someone like Wes, someone with an improbable, Forrest Gump kind of experiences: someone whose rifle is impeccably clean but can't hit anything with it, so he gets a shotgun instead; someone who sleeps through a mortar barrage that kills nearby tent-mates but comes out physically unscathed; someone whose peculiar sense of direction reveals their ship is going in a different way than they've been told, resulting in meeting the captain who confirms his insight but tells him to shut up about it.

When you finish reading, you'll find yourself wondering which is more improbable: Wes surviving the Marines, or the Marines surviving Wes.

Either way, it's a good ride and a great read!

— *David Reinhardt*

Prologue

Children are naturally born self-centered because they're the center of everything they perceive. Realizing the difference between oneself versus another occurs as a child grasps dependency, which in turn teaches give-and-take and conditioned responses. I wasn't different than other babies; when I cried, Mother came to my assistance.

Thus, the performance on my life stage began. Year after year, certain telling events triggered other events to prove and reprove how recognizing the value of all those *others* could in turn define oneself.

As a young teenager, I pictured others as either rebellious or acquiescent; bullies were rebels, and everyone else lived and let live. Once I got my driver's license, dichotomies evolved. Either you were the one who was looking or you were the one who was looked at, either a seeker or one who was sought. By eighteen, one was strong or weak, beautiful or ugly, a winner or a loser. It was about how one carried oneself that determined whether he or she thrived or merely survived. Then there were the haves and the have-nots—those who received and those who didn't. You were either my friend or my enemy.

Southeast Asia was a stewpot of wrath, brute will, and confusion. In the United States during the mid-1960s, chains of tradition were being tossed aside; conventional wisdoms wrestled with freedom of soul, choice, and long hair. "Don't just sit there, do something!" became tedious mantras from those with conspicuous prejudgments as opinions divided the population. Since no one was invading American soil, the military purpose in Vietnam was often ambiguous. A young person trying to decide what to do was not exactly well-defined.

As much as it had been a yes/no, black/white, or love/despise world to me, I began realizing maybes, grays, and balances. Moving toward compromises—that middle ground between mature and wishy-washy—captured my attention as a young adult. One still had to choose to be a participant, explore, choose again, and then learn. It didn't take long for the word *risk* to become a new companion concept along with its counterpoint consequences. Whenever I had a "what if" question about decisions, destinations, dangers, or inevitabilities, further "what if" questions were added to the list; most of these were never answered.

Nevertheless, it could be said everything up to this point in my life was nothing more than a repetitiously ordinary prologue to virtually anyone's chapter one. Perhaps it was, but to this end, I am forever reminded of a special place called Honalee.

Images Behind the Glass

Fall 1965

There are some amazing stories about the military. It can be that line in the sand so many of us young hunters cross, divorcing adulthood from youth. The military is not just marks in the sand, mind you; it's more like a creative array of strokes and strikes akin to conspicuous blue tattoos on our chests depicting our own brand or badge. It is a decisive decree indelibly inked for others to respect or at least recognize. For many, joining the armed forces legitimizes this particular point in time and choices just made.

Unless you're a wimp.

After all, we are ready for whatever comes our way, willing to take risks, convinced we are able, ready or not.

Nearly all of us, that is.

Arguably, the decision to sign up could be a public statement depicting machismo, significance, or physical prowess; however, it just as often can be an act of rebellion or escape. That decision to sign up often might be less about military purpose or patriotism than about an inevitable maturation event, an event introducing numerous subsequent choices and logical next steps.

Even if drafted, the armed forces can serve as beckoning open doors granting freedoms not experienced before or adventures to foreign places.

For so many, the military reveals a tattoo on the heart as well as the skin.

But what about all those what-if questions lurching through my brain?

Military purpose and patriotism are not trivial, of course; with the position comes cultural, public, and familial expectations. Yet, such principles are like the clothing we wear for people to see or even admire, not necessarily the muscles we build achieving more silent, salient, private objectives. Such personal choices refine the process and define he who chooses to take that next step.

At least that's what all those posters portrayed; anyone can see determination splashed across their faces. But I didn't know what I was supposed to do, or even what I *wanted* to do.

Of course it isn't the same for every person. Do we succumb to rules we're given, and then culturally comply? Do we travel roads less traveled just because. Do we ask no questions, choosing courses no one else might dare? Maybe we only do what's expected of us and merely become another public robot. Are these choices or absence of choices?

Expectations

Albuquerque was a good place to grow up. It was a big enough city, had friendly people, and I knew my way around. One day while confiding with my best friend, Steve, I realized university had become under-challenging. No, it wasn't easy or irrelevant necessarily, just not captivating. University was one choice among countless others, not unlike positioning cars in heavy traffic, knowing you must get from here to there, wherever *there* may be. I became jaded. While others gabbed about graduation requirements, I'd invisibly close my ears to justifications such as my Mother's, "You need school to get a good job," or all those teachers' repetitious renderings, "You'll get paid more money with a degree."

"What difference does it make what everybody else thinks?" Steve would badger me. "Just trust your gut." Without retorts from me, he continued, "Think what's behind the door. Don't you ever wonder about that?"

But everybody was already investing; my missing the point was an understatement! If it weren't for memorized responses, I'd have looked really stupid. You see, I could speak the right words, "I'm studying liberal arts" or "in eighteen months I'll be graduating" using well-scripted drafts. I just couldn't grasp implications so obvious to others. It was like I was living inside a disheartening fog.

Although I felt alone inside these self-commiserations, I wasn't disappointing anyone else.

Institutions of Higher Learning

Another prickly, lingering billboard: duty.

Although I didn't think I was capable, I was actually close to earning a degree, so within the family, it was definitely expected. Perhaps they sought to celebrate something they personally had wanted, so surely I would do what they could not or had not done. This yoke was familial duty, and I of course accepted the assignment, oh *so* dutifully, as the right thing to do.

I was prepared to respond to questions like, "What are you studying?" or, "What are your career choices?" First: "I'm studying anthropology." Having worked two summers on a field crew employed by *the* Smithsonian in Montana under my belt always caught an ear and fit my blue jeans character. This experience brought many "Oh, really?" kind of remarks, making me feel good. Sometimes I'd answer more obliquely, "I'm planning to be a professor" because it sounded appropriate among family and friends. Having stacks of history books on my shelf, responses like, "So logical!" stalked behind these synthetic conversations. That word "logical" made me feel it was indeed a logical choice.

Although Steve lettered in only one sport, he was still proud to wear his "H" letter-jacket until he graduated from Highland High School that spring; after all, it was a badge of achievement. He'd explain, "Parents give pride, guys give respect, girls give attention, so that 'H' gives me rank. What else is there besides what people believe you to be?"

Steve had things figured out.

But for me, my indecisiveness became demoralizing. Maybe I did know but hadn't yet made very good choices, like whether to study harder or quit, to get a job or join the navy, to save money or buy the right things. Isn't it about time I did? Steve was more decisive; that fall he quit University, turning that page without looking back.

One afternoon we were talking about a bunch of what-if questions when I said "Sometimes, I just can't make up my mind. There are so many choices."

To that he said, "Would you rather be judged by the risks you took, or for never having made any mistakes at all?"

Steve was a ready, smiling, unshackled teenager prepared for anything; there was no doubt there'd be no more academics for him!

Elephant in the Room

Meanwhile, Vietnam hung midair like a slow-moving fan going around and around, cooling no one while we sweated. College colleagues affirmed how inconvenient going to Vietnam could be. Besides, it was dangerous. Some guys went to Canada to avoid the draft. Others stayed in school to assure draft deferments. Inside the student union lounge, anti-war chats were common. Let the Green Berets and camouflaged uniforms protect us so we can do what we want, like drink beer, drive fast, pick up chicks, and stay out all night.

Grown-up-type freedoms competed for our attention. Students voiced their opinions aloud and in printed headlines and editorials. Steve and I vigorously reaffirmed similar conversations over full ashtrays and empty glasses four to eight times a week as we explored a variety of options; but, we always seemed to come back to someone in a uniform. Some girls never quite got it, but we could agree they were sure good at listening to these conversations and smiling at the same time.

After Steve withdrew from the University of New Mexico, he fixated on his own next step in a heartbeat. He and I began talking endlessly about the military. Our exchanges conjured images resembling comic book dramas; we began living on aircraft carriers, flying helicopters or jet planes, and driving tanks. While we knew we might not likely ever *do* these things, we identified with the possibility nonetheless. We let our eyes linger on all those recruiting posters.

Meanwhile, when I was by myself I wrestled with being a piano player, climbing mountains, or becoming a teacher like Mom wanted. Even better, I could be that *National Geographic* explorer or *New York Times* journalist I actually dreamed about. Choosing which ideas to ponder or which to dismiss overwhelmed me, so I let them stack up in my head like unopened letters. They troubled me and infected my more traditionally set outlook based on family, old photographs, and scrapbook fairytales.

Smoke and beer became comfort foods. Daily nicotine chats with Steve led to more what-if dialogues for a couple of months. We both desperately needed the other's opinion to form our own. I'd say "what if" and he'd say "why not?" My desert mind began to focus on water and ships. Steve considered heavy weapons, war movies, boots, and blazes. I thought about charting oceans; he about John Wayne. I thought of tides; he thought of targets. Courageous daydreaming competed with practical realities, but neither won.

Partying out late meant sleeping in. Ah, all the forgotten dreams.

We also discussed decision-making itself. What would parents and others say? But we didn't talk about a military purpose as depicted by politicians in *Time Magazine* and never about actually killing anyone. We never even talked about anything negative such as our chances of *being* killed. Instead, we zeroed in on adventure, exotic places, being independent, and making one's mark.

The military was a means to an end. It was the real ticket, a tangible license. It was grabbing hold of us, tugging.

Grappling Prime Time

Behind our eyes, risk itself became immaterial. Freedom was common ground, although Steve and I never used this word in our commiserations. Untying those binding ropes that held us back would take something stronger.

It was early November when Steve became irritatingly impatient; he couldn't find a job. I just earned a failing grade on my German midterm with two other Ds halfway through the semester. My C-plus-iosis disorder festered into C-minus-iosis. This may have been private, but it hid an educational secret I had to divulge soon enough. Like infections, academics festered like wounds failing to heal.

Was I lazy or restless?

In August I had purchased a yellow '65 Mustang 289 High Performance that had four on the floor, a black interior, and it was fast. Payments made it tough to buy gas, but I was frugal. I liked the image but not the expense. I liked being attractive to those who looked at me, and yet I didn't like feeling shallow. Jangling keys in my pocket made me feel important; little else did.

I once thought I had things figured out when I was making those As and Bs; the world was mine to seize. Why couldn't I figure out what to do now? I felt smart. I felt dumb. It used to be that any mountain might be worth the climb. Grownup challenges were now mine to conquer. At twenty-one I now felt either fifteen or twenty-five without being able to confirm which.

Meanwhile my part-time job at Continental Airlines ended (they closed down operations), and I transferred to TWA as a telephone robot in a room full of programmed androids. We memorized scripts so we didn't have to think. I smiled so my voice would sound happy. I showed up on time and went home on time. I took fifteen-minute breaks.

Why can't I scratch this itch?

Didn't I have any sense of accountability and willingness to take some risks? Not being able to make decisions,

I suddenly began to feel guilty trivializing expectations among those who mattered most, like my family.

While watching helicopters and tanks on the news doing formidable stuff, Steve and I stared at magnetic depictions of rugged soldiers with resolute faces. Our exhaling became heavy and deep. Our eyes focused and our eyebrows narrowed. We spoke the same language as those soldiers. Change was imminent. We were ripe.

Fork in the Road

November 1965

Choices were considered amid anxieties of the unknown and hours of deliberation. Steve was becoming preoccupied. "I just don't want to do something halfway, dammit." I wasn't able to detect where that particular sentence would lead next as he stared at the ceiling. "I gotta find a job that pays enough 'cuz I want to buy a car. And, I don't want to work at McDonalds."

He wanted the right car to impress his girlfriend I thought. He talked about becoming a state trooper, or an auto mechanic, or just joining the army. I wasn't grasping what his wanting to *go all the way* meant. I said "Road cops earn good bucks, and people pay attention to you!" I knew more about what he didn't want than what he did, which was twice as much as I knew about my own wants.

"Let's join the marines, the *U*nited States Marine Corps," Steve declared one afternoon as he underlined the letter "U" to evoke a "you" as he pointed his finger at me. His eyes plied for decisiveness not only on my part, but his own as well. His jaw tightened.

I had trouble grasping the full image as I stood on the edge of this never before contemplated precipice, wondering if this bent-kneed wimp who was wearing my clothes had guts to jump. My knee jerked in self contemplation. I asked, "Do you think we got what it takes?" I wondered about my own physical prowess while licking my front teeth. I felt that C-minus infirmity creeping in, that lingering malady festering further as of late.

I could sprint a mile, but it's not like I could win a marathon. I could dribble a basketball, but seldom do a swish. It wasn't that I didn't have my own bag of skills; mine were just not physical. After all, I could type 70 wpm, but guys didn't type fast in those days or admit it if they did. Heck, I even knew shorthand; not a single guy I knew could do that (I rationalized it useful for taking class notes; it wasn't). Nobody thought anybody who liked maps as much as I did or who was good in geography was good at very much else.

Indeed I tended to believe most folks about most things. But how could such feeble skills be used? Was I going to be no more than a tall scrawny kid easily shoved aside in a crowd of athletes? I had come to an unsupportable conclusion I was the epitome of wheelchair mediocrity. Maybe I wasn't disabled, just disenabled and pushed around by others who seemed to have already figured things out. So here I remained seated.

People with direction were all around doing the right stuff, good stuff, intended stuff—nothing accidental. I felt purpose in my friends' handshakes and in their eyes as they left for school in another state or got good jobs. Intruding into every conversation, these people leaned forward, looked seriously, and gripped intensely.

In my mind, I was paused alongside an enticing cliff barely able to see water below. I was almost sure there *was* water down there, and almost sure that if I dove in I could position a dive to survive. The test here became the choice to remain alive or to live dead. Indecisiveness competed with improbability.

Blood brothers

"OK, let's do it," I affirmed to Steve that very day.

Ignoring self-imposed frailties that I may have convinced myself to bear, this unknown lure seemed the right thing to do whether it was or not. The cliff was still there and the breaths still deep, but there was something new: the willingness to close one's eyes, jump, and to take what came. That joining the military may be a worthy goal unto itself no longer mattered; changing my attitude toward doing something worthy, was.

Steve's raised eyes met mine. Slapping palms, we grasped hands and gave each other a look that needed no further words. We touched each other's pulse to validate the commitments we were making. I recall creating a mental image about how he and I had just cut our palms. Our hands bled and imaginary blood oozed out from between our palms. We shook hands and shared blood.

The exchange produced a permanent bond like those seen in movies. As trite as it sounds, the mental confirmation of this bond was honest and heartfelt.

For me it was a decision made.

We went to the recruiting office together and signed up the second week of November; there were signs posted that the Marine Corps birthday was coming up the next day, the tenth. Neither of us asked permission. When I had to make purposeful decisions in the past, I'd always seek parental consent and blessing beforehand. Not this time. We signed the final papers. Tangible orders would be ready on November 16; but that day, the ninth, was the point of no return. Physical exams were scheduled for November 12th. As long as there were no medical obstacles to prevent it, we'd leave Albuquerque on November 17th. These acts now started to fall one at a time like dominos. I stood taller, felt manly, and leaned a bit forward when I walked.

The same afternoon I went to the used car lot and sold my Mustang. Receiving enough to pay off the loan with about $100 left over, I told my mother I'd joined the marines. I gave her the $100 to pay off some bills. The only thing she said was, "Are you *sure* about this?" as she turned her head away hiding her eyes. That night, I recollect hearing her moan and cry all night, it seemed. I couldn't sleep anyhow.

The next morning was a melancholy breakfast without words. After Dad had left for work, Mom asked a solemn one word question, "When?" Her chin touched her neck. She didn't want to look right at me.

The question lingered heavily until I finally revealed, "the seventeenth." My voice trailed off with that *point-of-no-return* kind of dismissal.

"So soon," she quavered. Her eyes released more tears and pressed into palms. It was like someone had died; her hands covered her face. She knew I was serious.

I sought something to say and after a long pause continued, "It's better not to linger around. I have enough time to withdraw from school, get rid of a few things. It'll work."

That evening, Dad didn't ask any questions at all. He did say how hurt my mother felt and how she had so many higher expectations, but he never did tell me how *he* felt. I guess I never knew how he really felt about anything thinking back on all the, "Yes, dears" and all the kind but indifferent remarks. On the other hand, I was privately pleased for his acquiescence and respect for my decision without argument or admonishments. Brother Paul had no opinion. He gave me a whatever-you-want response.

I next called Grandmother. She thoughtfully asked if I had made up my mind; I said I had. Then she said, "Good!" I understood this instantly as approval for the act of deciding, not necessarily about the decision itself. She was less surprised than I would have imagined. Then she said something odd I had not anticipated, "Y'know, Wesley, a decision well-made or ill-made is a firm decision nonetheless. One learns over time that certain kinds of decisions affect numerous other decisions along the way as well as numerous other people. But, whatever you do, *never decide not to decide*. Know that I love you, and that in my heart I know you *will* do well at what you choose to do." This particular domino I hadn't anticipated. She always knew more than she disclosed, but she disclosed no dismay, no grandmotherly advice, and no other precautionary words.

Physical exams on November 12 were medically thorough. Recollecting a doctor's visit ten years prior, I remember Mom being overly concerned about my heart murmur. Although there was never therapy or medications, it was something I was supposed to keep track of since it could be potentially serious in the future, but the subject never came up during those ten years prior. During the physical, this memory came back. Detecting irregular heartbeats during this final hurdle now at age twenty-one would disqualify me. I was short of panicking but still alarmed; but, the doctor didn't detect any murmurs. I sped through evaluation lines along with the rest of the athletes, rebels, and marine wannabes.

There were no further obstacles, no opinions by family or friends extended, and not much last-minute advice besides a couple whispered "Be careful" and, "Take care of yourself" in my ears, along with Mom's prolonged hugs and a good home-cooked dinner in my honor the night before. I counted on objections but witnessed resignations instead. New ground. We were long past acts of persuasion. Everyone looked at me with different eyes.

Tracking West

The seventeenth came. Wearing old clothes I would

never wear again, we convened at the train station early and stood outside in front of the Santa Fe Depot, Alvarado Hotel, and Fred Harvey Restaurant where I used to wait for the El Capitan train, which seemed like ages ago.

It was strange how uneventful such an eventful day turned out to be. It was such a significant demarcation line being crossed, yet I merely was traveling west instead of east on the very same train I took each summer to visit Grandma ten years ago. I felt like a young child with his eyes wide open. Suddenly, I didn't feel any taller, or older, any more mature, or much more educated. I guess my parents looked older as they restrained their cringes. Everyone forced appropriate smiles to publicly honor my decision. The cool November morning air lingered around our restrained stares and glances. We needed distance. Albuquerque would never be the same.

Steve's parents were there but a ways away. As the train lugged in slowed, and then hissed, the two families merged, looking like they didn't really expect to see the other. A few appropriately polite words were exchanged.

Two mothers had teary, wet faces. They extended their sons' hugs and uttered some drawn-out unintelligible utterings. There surely must've been lots more words in those five minutes. When did those things slip out of memory?

The thump-thump, thump-thump and squealing metallic screeches carried away this twenty-one year old to foreign destinations not completely comprehended or fully appreciated. Grandma's "decision well-made or ill-made" comment kept returning to my ears. Still, those nascent feelings of duty competed against other compelling dichotomies, whizzing through my head: self versus other, guilt versus responsibility, child versus adult. On the other hand, this heady, testosterone-primed, forward-leaning sensation seduced me; it grabbed my soul, tugged my gut, and focused my eyes. I yielded willingly, abducted by an adolescent's lust for his own life.

The invisible line was now crossed. No rebellion. No irresponsible act. It was, however, a *sliver of self* emerging from a youthful cocoon, a cocoon nurtured by others for a long time to get to this point, but unraveling this particular day for the first time.

This was more than a mere decision; I had finally made a rather decisive life choice.

Contemplative Journey

It took a couple of hours before Steve and I had regular conversations; after all, it was easy to sightsee red cliffs approaching Gallup and avoid internal introspections. We moved on as if we were riding horseback to points unknown on our own, saddlebags packed and bellies full.

"So whadaya think?" I asked Steve as we entered Arizona and sipped Cokes in the dome car. Steve hadn't been on a train before, and we had just finished exploring all the cars. I told him a couple stories about taking trains to Chicago, and how I lingered between the cars to get fresh air and listen to the train wheels. I was expecting some verbal, adventure-oriented affirmations.

"I didn't expect my Mom to cry so much," he said thoughtfully. "She always gets so worked up about things, but she told me she knew I'd do just fine."

Steve wasn't a particularly emotional guy like this, so it was easy for me to admit mine cried too. We traded our touring mood for more serious exchanges.

"But my Dad sure liked the idea!" His mood became upbeat.

I couldn't say the same. "I guess I am getting a little nervous about tomorrow; I'm not sure what to expect." I hoped to steer the issue away from people we left behind.

"My Dad never says much, but when he does, he knows exactly what to say. I thought he'd just tell me to 'give 'em hell' or 'don't kiss any ass,' but instead he said I made him proud." Steve juggled two different parental cautions. "Yeah, *proud*! My Dad never told me *that* before.

And you know what moms are like, right?" Steve sounded like he felt blessed.

"I know what you mean." My mom cried as well, but it wasn't the same, and no one ever said they were proud of *me*. I didn't want to exhibit any sadness or regret right then, so I went along with Steve's turnaround fervor, the kind of animation he always liked me to witness. He passed through his reflective mood and once again became gung ho. I believe he knew exactly what I was thinking and what to do when I became sullen.

Depots

A day and a half later, our train ride finally ended in San Diego; Steve and I were greeted by two uniformed men who politely herded us and a half dozen others onto a government bus destined for Marine Corps Recruit Depot (MCRD) located on the harbor north of downtown and adjacent to the airport. Off-the-wall mental gymnastics began as we approached the MCRD gates with trepidation. Not being fully prepared, intimidation now seemed to mount over the most trivial things.

Trying to look back over five decades, my mind now zigzags, bashing down alleys littered with tin-can observations amid dirty, oily passages strewn with newspaper headlines now appearing in my grandkids' history books. My zigzagging recollections recall the obligatory process of having to scrape off twenty years of cultural scabs, dismissing givens from teachers and preachers, learning how to salute stars and stripes, and even enjoying mass-produced food proffered by overweight NCOs wearing filthy aprons. But this initial intimidation was not necessarily fear-based, rather it was an eye-opening, anxiety-prodding venture akin to parachuting out a plane, not knowing exactly where you'd land.

I didn't know it then but how I embraced things over the next few years would be different than others, even Steve. I've listened to so many other stories of strategy and tactics, of medals and heroism, of purpose and practice, that I now understand my journey was not particularly parallel to anyone else's that I know about.

My story is better described as a recounting of unanticipated events. It is how raw spirit reacted to what it saw for the first time. It wasn't at all "gung ho" like Steve's; it was more about curiosity and exploration, about what was being etched on my virgin soul that inevitably followed marching through those doors.

3

Uniform Culture

November 1965 – January 1966

Our heads were buzzed in twenty seconds. All of our coifs were consistent, looking like identical twins. Personalities disappeared. Once naked in line to take the first shower, our civvies were removed from benches, so we were told, and sent "back to where they came from." We never saw them again. There was a sudden feeling of having nothing left of our own, nothing to connect us to who we once were or where we came from. There was nothing but our most basic animal form without status or style or any human pretense among a herd of other, similar flesh.

A new towel would be waiting for us after hot water blasting, soaping, and rinsing, and then we'd be off to a warehouse with stacks of clothing. Three T-shirts here, three jockey shorts there, three pants here, three utility shirts all emerged in predictable patterns. Our "wardrobe to go" came in three sizes: medium, large and extra-large. Our arms and shoulders weighed down with strange Clorox-like scents as each of us picked a wad of three athletic socks and stuffed them into pillowcases. DIs (drill instructors) yelled at every one of us not to go so slowly, not to drop anything, not to talk, not to, not to . . .

Circling the steamy room, we immediately changed from wearing wet towels to dry underwear and T-shirts. The floor was slippery cement, yet we had to hop on one leg while writhing our other leg through the opening, keeping the stuffed pillowcase under an arm or over shoulders (and off the wet floor). Then we had to keep moving toward a narrow room full of boots, shoes, and sneakers amid DI's corrugated shouting.

One at a time, each guy was instructed to holler his shoe size request with a "sir" at the beginning and end of each and every sentence, I recall "Sir! 10 D, sir!" or "Sir! 10½ wide, sir!" or "Sir! 11 E, sir!" being most common. The staff marine then banged the black boots, dress shoes, and sneakers onto a wooden countertop with a deliberate wild clunk. Upon reaching the target zone, I yelled "Sir, 14 A, sir!" The sergeant behind the counter winced. Was it the "14" or was it the "A"?

"Stand over there!" He snarled. I compliantly joined another guy (towering 6'6", maybe more), a black football player-type guy who wore a size fifteen extra wide. Out of eighty of us in line, only he and I were singled out for peculiar feet. The grainy leather boots we received were different and not polished smooth black like all the others'. One of the staff's side comments was that these were leftovers from World War II. They didn't make our size anymore, something like that; I wasn't sure if true, but the boots were definitely odd and old. Though coarsely rough to touch, they were off-black with a slightly green, shiny luster. Riding higher up the leg, they had more laces, a more rounded heel, and fit snug around the lower calf. However, we received standard-issue sneakers and dress shoes. Both of us were issued a *standard* wide size; it would have to do. I'd just tie my laces tighter. The footwear worked out, but someone could write a book about my feet; guys just didn't have ultra-narrow feet.

Once sufficiently garbed, we dropped off our stuffed pillowcases in our barracks, dressed, exited, and were immediately exercised. We ran, did push-ups, sit-ups, ran some more, and marched to near exhaustion. Everything we were taught was taught for the team: how to think collectively, how to think for the other person, and how to think for the platoon mission.

Once, we were warned we were having a uniform inspection. To communicate teamwork, we had to critically evaluate others in the platoon to a fault. We'd evaluate everything from slightly askew shirt creases to a tad of toothpaste on a lower lip. DIs were relentless in finding just one more little point until our own level of critique became just as relentless. We indeed began finding specks of lint on our shirts or dust on a shoe. But it was never enough.

One day after showers, we stood naked, the DI halted our clump of guys to tell us we had failed inspection from the day before. He cited a list of trivial misdeeds, like a belt hanging incorrectly, a shirt wrinkle, and shaving omissions. Then he said we would now have a second chance. This time, however, specific instructions were to shave the face of our partner to perfection, then to personally inspect *his* shoes, shirt, belts, and pants and he ours as if a DI would. Hell was the reward for whoever missed something amiss on his partner.

Amid a few residual red scratched necks below taut jaw lines and frowning eyes, we passed the test with an ever so mild compliment from the DI. We achieved the platoon's mission after all.

Hands-On Training

Later on we practiced how to climb knotted ropes. Making sure boots or sneakers caught the knot was troublesome, but eventually we all made it up bumpy white ropes, some quicker than others. If you didn't make it to the top, everyone else had to do ten or twenty push-ups, but not *you!* Instead, *you* were given a second chance (and admonition) to climb. If *you* didn't make it to the top again, everyone else had to do even more push-ups. This was supposed to give incentive to recruits to try even harder. It didn't always work.

When it didn't, sometimes the slouch would receive physical incentives from bunkmates after dark. The justice of this didn't seem fair, but in the end everybody did make it to the top of the knotted ropes. Gratifying to me, I was not at the very bottom of any of those "bad lists." However, was my "C-plus-iosis" kicking back in? My rope-climbing spirit waned as my skinny arm muscles simply couldn't lift the weight. I must learn to try harder.

Then we started climbing ropes *without* knots—problematic for quite a few, me included. We all did extra push-ups for each guy not making it up the rope, which made my arms even less able when my turn came. Now there were seven or eight of us who didn't have enough muscle (or too much weight) to gain that top rung.

After scores of penalty push-ups, the DI bellowed sarcastically, "OK, ladies, how are we going to resolve this problem?" After a panicky pause, that 15-wide black football player stood up and approached the overweight guy not making progress then kneeled as he pulled up on the guy's heels so he could position them onto his own shoulders. He lifted his own knees from a squat. The overweight climber edged upward with the white cable loose-knitted in his crotch, and his ankles compressing the rope. Fright in his eyes, he inched up until he made it.

We all glanced from left to right and squinted with lips pursed in restrained smiles of mutual satisfaction that the DI didn't demand another alternative; we wanted to cheer. During my turn, a similar thing occurred; I made it up with the same heels-on-shoulder maneuver. But after touching the crossbeam about twenty feet up, I stiffened. I had trouble with heights. My eyes blurred with gut-grabbing acrophobia followed by a panicked stop.

"You did it! C'mon, slide down!" a couple guys shouted, "just let go!"

Blindly, I did, and then stopped a fast descent by clutching the rope with my free right hand. I gripped hard, ripping the skin *entirely* off from my right ring finger and then falling flat onto sand. Blood oozed all over. White flaps of skin peeled back around my finger. About an inch of bone was visible covered with a thick, pasty looking, white film. The DI was not at all pleased but called a corpsman. We walked to sick bay so I could get fixed up. I had to hold my right hand tightly shoehorned inside my left fist, letting the finger dribble. I disguised wincing with clenched teeth.

After the lead corpsman used standard techniques to clean my wound thoroughly and prepare my finger by removing dead skin, he thickly smeared on gooey medication, gauzed it up, bandaged it into a fat hot dog-sized dressing, and sent me back to my unit. Relieved of having to do certain basic things, like swimming, I was firmly reminded that not passing physical tests would hold me back and boot camp would start over for me in a new platoon. Though I can swim, I'm unsure it was officially noted that I never did go through swimming tests.

Dreading any possibility of getting held back, I religiously committed to preventing it by having my bandages changed twice daily at meal times so I wouldn't miss training or classes. Some finger tissue was lost, and a whitish film formed over bone, thickening into genuine tissue. Unexpectedly, they never stitched the wound instead letting skin reform over newly congealed undertissue. It didn't bleed much after the initial tear; they kept it liberally covered with gooey ointment for weeks. It didn't even hurt that much either except when I applied pressure or when I bathed in hot water. To this day, I have a jagged, prickly sensitivity on this finger. Curiously, almost no fingerprint exists on my right ring finger, a multi-decade reminder of this odd event.

Less than two weeks into our mind-cleansing, physically-demanding indoctrinations, Thanksgiving became a day of physical and mental mercy. Turkey was served. Anyone wanting to attend church could. Going to church was always a good option on Sundays as a reprieve from normal daily training hullabaloos. For some, it was an added chance to doze discreetly. That week we had an extra Sunday on Thursday!

4

Summoning Summits

January 1966

Without making unnecessary self-deprecating remarks, it's safe to say I probably ranked pretty low on the physical skills scale. Others could do more sit-ups or push-ups or pull-ups than I, and there were several times they exerted extra push-ups on behalf of my shortcomings. Besides having my finger to contend with, there was little doubt I was one of the skinniest out of eighty with only a couple overweight guys behind me on the prowess charts. Steve was much further up these scales than I and thriving. My self-esteem had a hard time keeping pace.

On the other hand, after scoring very well on multiple-choice exams, I willingly accepted the job mentoring others on Marine Corps history, and basic rules and regulations. Even though I had trouble crawling under barbed wire, my highbrow coaching strengths offered some balance and maybe a "push up" others needed.

Mid-December, we learned one guy among us was to be elected recruit leader. Whoever it was would receive extra duties for creating morale incentives for us to act like a team (and a few extra privileges for the effort). In addition, he would gain the rank of private first class (PFC) upon graduation from MCRD when the rest of us gained the rank of private. He had to be strong enough to shout and actually *cause* us to willingly and dutifully respond. He'd need to be someone to look up to with behaviors we could emulate.

In our platoon, there was this full-sized athletic black guy named Kearse who repeatedly singled himself out with muscular competence. There was no real competition; he got the job. He commanded us in various physical activities, exercise routines, and escorted us daily to chow while the DI walked nearby to observe his leadership. Kearse thrived proudly as a black leader among predominantly white recruits during a time of evolving civil rights. Such recognition probably caught some folks' eyes.

Parade Ground Rules

One of Kearse's responsibilities was to bear our Marine Corps pennant by carrying it in front whenever we, Platoon #1026, marched around the grounds. These were organized marches in formation with stops and starts as well as all the other routine maneuvers like about-faces (making a 180 degree turn), salutes to officers or the flag, and at-eases (where we remained standing in a resting stance with arms behind our backs). Kearse gained our respect even though he kept us busy doing *something* during virtually every spare moment we weren't in class, cleaning rifles, eating, doing push-ups, showering, or in the john. Kearse was not the nasty drill instructor he could have been; by this time we did indeed want to be an effective team.

Christmas passed like Thanksgiving—without fanfare except a big meal with choices of meat and cranberry sauce plus another extra Sunday midweek. Opportunities to gain reprieve from daily ordeals by attending church were seized again.

Kearse led us Protestants to a chapel where Christmas services and communion led by Lutheran ministers was conducted. However, if one weren't Lutheran, you were excluded from taking communion. It was only grape juice, but it did seem odd to omit any of us from participation. Why did Lutherans do this? Still, while I safely speculated most guys were not overtly religious, no one missed juice or unsalted crackers.

Tides of Strides

New Year's Day came and went almost unnoticed.

Next to the last week of boot camp and right after another series of prophetic warnings from a DI about how my finger could be affecting my ability to graduate, we were all jogging very hard down the beach as a group—a final endurance test of sorts. Running in soft sand was doubly difficult with T-shirts massaging our pecs, causing two bloody spots amidst the sweat for many. Plus, this was the first time we were pushing our lungs for a deliberate grueling march over a long distance literally for four hours in an outdoor oven.

Kearse was having trouble. As muscular as he was, his failure to exhibit extended endurance was showing. I had been initially positioned near the rear because I ran with the other less-athletic guys. This last batch was composed of those bearing lowest expectations, those who wouldn't slow down others but still had to finish. Prodded to keep up or at least not falter *too* far back, one lone nudging DI chaperoned these dozen aberrants.

It became a long, olive-green, snake-like string of jogging recruits—a sludge fest of one hundred sixty sandy sneakers spreading footprints upon footprints on wet beach aprons, muddy sand that further impeded our speed.

We all dripped with sweat, showing fatigue. One recruit fell and a DI stopped with him. We learned later he had heatstroke and remained in sick bay two days before rejoining us. Others stumbling were persuaded to get back up and keep going as our serpentine line of now seventy-nine stretched and extended.

The sun was ruthless as we perspired rhythmically. Our drained pace was slowing, elongating to a football field in length. Moving down beach, Kearse slipped and our banner hit the sand with a thump; he recovered on his own, but struggled a second time. Thinking he would fall out, a recruit behind him picked up the flapping red pennant and took lead position as Kearse faded into mid-ranks inconspicuously. By then I had gained position joining the main clump of runners in the middle.

As we dizzily trounced along, trips and falls into the sand suddenly became common. The DIs finally slowed pace but relentlessly kept hollering as they too sweltered alongside, encouraging the now trudging momentum not to cease. This was their mission! This was *our* mission!

Our now less structured, seventy-nine, grim-faced, almost-marines lengthened even more as quite a few could not keep up the unyielding struggle, but for some reason I *could*! I passed Steve mid-pack and then Kearse! Hot and sweaty but with second wind securely in place, I held a regular trudging pace and gained row by row until eventually I approached the actual front of the pack. The standard fell for the fourth time, but this time it was I who picked it up.

After miles and miles of hard slogging, our extended caterpillar-like entourage was within a half mile of the now visible endpoint. All seventy-nine remaining guys in this rather loose, maybe hundred yards plus long bedraggled parade were still in forced-march mode (like a slow jog) but slowing down to a labored half-fast plod. With the real end in sight, we knew we were going to make it. Yet it was I who carried the platoon's red and gold colors across that final finish line a full ten feet ahead of the next runner. Yes, my heart was thumping with genuine Semper fi pride for the first time.

But my finish also raised eyebrows among certain others. I had been labeled one least likely to last—a bottom-of-the-list kind of marine. Despite a finger injury and physical limitations compared to football players and Adonis lookalikes, I sensed an unspoken respect toward me among DIs that day. They didn't become softer, but they didn't push me with the same bias they had against others who were overweight or underperforming. I also exceeded my own expectations that day; it had been an "A plus" day! My heavily bandaged finger that prevented officially passing swimming maneuvers didn't prevent me from running or graduating after all.

Despite quirky hurdles, I made the grade. I unconsciously stood about an inch taller. Sometimes, I feel this event caused me to have a few conceited thoughts about what really counts in boot camp, but admittedly I didn't have very many other events that produced similar reflections. Was my head a little swollen from outperforming the "best of 'em"? Or was my outlook somehow merging into a group of other selfless spirits that day?

No matter. William Kearse was promoted to PFC as anticipated, standing proud at graduation holding the platoon's standard as he gained rank to Private First Class and new collar rank insignias in public ceremony. This L.A.-based marine stood tall and smiled with gratification having achieved this breakthrough recognition.

Everyone else earned their first stripe and thus officially became a real private in the United States Marine Corps with a detectable pride only we could identify.

All of us eyeballed the parade ground that day, scrutinizing other raw platoons of eighty recruits learning to march amid high-pitched DI commands...eighty wrinkled, unrhythmic newbies appearing quite loose within their ranks, adolescent in their untrained eyes, and untailored in their public exhibitions. *But not us!*

They trudged and paraded near us "real marines" who were bearing this newly blessed sense of I-can-do-it manly pride as authentic members of *the* team. This was not just any team, mind you. It was *our* team who had just validly earned a gracious smugness...a legitimate self-importance coupled with what would ultimately become lifelong ties to others similarly festooned.

Specialties and Realities

Steve and I went on to ITR (Infantry Training Regiment) at Camp Pendleton along with the others for four more weeks of rifle training, target practice, grenade-throwing, and field exercises, carrying weapons in much more adverse conditions and antagonistic settings. ITR was weapons skills, and I wasn't particularly adept at hitting the target, though my rifle was impeccably clean. Boot camp had been rigorous, vigorous, and demanding beyond my normal abilities. I survived perhaps more based on my attitude rather than ability.

Each weekend we got either Friday or Saturday off and headed for Oceanside on our first leaves; I was twenty-one and legal! The bandage on my finger was much less conspicuous by now too.

Steve and I were assigned to different units because of our skill sets and choices. I elected to enter admin training because I could use a typewriter (a rare skill among new marines), followed by a unique four more weeks at Vietnamese language school after acing the military language aptitude test—a remarkable surprise noted by both of my sergeants-in-charge. Steve and I pledged to keep in touch as these separate doors began to open.

Having gained twenty pounds in twenty weeks, I weighed a healthy one hundred seventy pounds. I felt like a different person not only physically but mentally as well.

Spiritual graduation

Once I learned how to march and salute and walk like a marine, I stood tall, having achieved something unanticipated. My self-imposed "A" grade gave me personal victories on two fronts: one for achieving something worthy I had almost convinced myself I could never do, and another for gaining the right to be on the Marine Corps team. I now had the privilege to use those private words "Semper fi" that marines use to recognize each other, special words that mean *always faithful* — faithful to the United States of America, to the Corps, and to each other.

Although I didn't embody the ooh-rah vigor or the bristling musculature of most graduates, I was a passenger on the same train. I had my internal tattoo, was ready for the next pages to turn...ripe for where they might lead to next.

5

Hacking Military Secrets With A Paper Sextant

Summer 1966

After boot camp, infantry training, admin school, Vietnamese language school, a month of leave visiting parents and friends in New Mexico, and a shepherded check-in rigmarole at the United States Marine Base in San Diego, I successfully reported for duty late June. Ready for the unknowns as I ever would be, I showed up spiffy, perfect in uniform, and focused in attitude as I leaned just a little forward with each deliberate step; plus I had a stripe on my arms! It was easier being prepared for unknowns than it was for things too well defined or specifically bad, especially among others who also fed upon those same unknowns.

In the peaceful harbor were three prominent gray ships: the Iwo Jima (or "Iwo" for short), the Thomaston, and my ship the Vancouver, all silently and ominously anchored as guardians of the bay after arriving back from the Far East that previous week. I stared at little else.

Warships Arrive Home

Three San Diego-based amphibious force warships, from left, Iwo Jima, Vancouver and Thomaston — steam toward Point Loma. Three ships were homeward-bound after nine months in Vietnam waters. The vessels docked at the Naval Station yesterday. They sailed from the harbor 9, 1966. The Coronado Islands are in background.

Announcing our three ships coming into port.

Since embarkation was 3:00 PM, later that morning I walked pensively into a nearby residential neighborhood to soak in life as I avoided the cracks in the sidewalks (Mom's back would be thankful). I examined the odd detail of the cement; its usual mundaneness suddenly became meaningful. Mailboxes, tidy yards with neatly trimmed bushes, grease residues in driveways, and gum wrappers in the gutters captured my eyes. I lingered for two hours, taking it in. I guess it was a private farewell to civilization as I knew it before the trek.

I finally returned past entry gate MPs to survey those shipyard guardians. While making sure I was mentally primed to board, I dutifully waited in line and deliberated new doors, both literally and figuratively, swinging open in front of me.

Finding my gear amidst staged mounds of green duffels, I boarded on time, thinking we'd be on our way shortly. However, the trio of ships was silent except for clinkings and clunkings of bags and boots loading onboard and strange, hollow echoes of metal against metal. Day after day, I witnessed more and more cargo loading from pallets of wrapped boxes to genuine, brand new shiny helicopters. Every other day we went ashore into nearby San Diego and hit local bars or crossed into Tijuana, making sure we returned by curfews created by the last water shuttle to our ship. Stories proliferated among us getting back on time about trouble others got into who accidentally missed the last boat.

The Iwo was a huge hulking LPH (Landing Platform Harbor). Like bees buzzing around a hive, I watched the choppers flying into the side of the Iwo (at least that's what I always wanted to think—they actually landed on top using lifts to go up and down).

The two smaller ships, LPDs (Landing Platform Docks), were troop carriers, but they too had platforms top deck where choppers came and went. The Twenty-Sixth Marine Regiment, or just "Twenty-Sixth Marines," was assigned to the USS Vancouver.

Looking from our ship, the Vancouver, toward the "Iwo" with its helicopter mouth.

We lived on board about a week before finally departing San Diego the first week of July. We sailed right into the sunset with half of us lingering toward the bow. Half of us studied bright yellow western unknowns and the other half studied the fading skyline of San Diego skyscrapers to the east.

At sea, officers kept us active at PT (physical training) on deck or busy in classes. Occasionally some of us flew in one of the helicopters to attend special training programs onboard one of the other ships. Choppers scuttled back and forth during the day frequently, either for hauling troops or for pilot practice. It was always fascinating to watch them flying into the side or on top like enormous insects buzzing around and then entering their nests.

Close-up from the Vancouver, we could see where the choppers rested during transit.

We slept in very tight quarters with less than two feet between bunks, so tight that when one guy rolled over, he'd push up on the marine in the bunk above. People breathed, snored, coughed, and sneezed nonstop, but it took only a couple of days at sea to discover how to ignore these sounds.

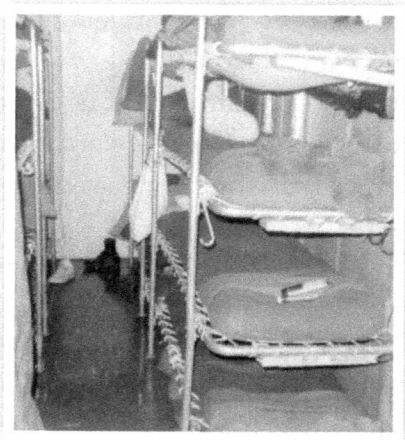

Tight quarters.

With ample free time for movies, card playing, walking around, socializing, or writing letters, I checked out the big wall map of the world on bridge deck. As I was grasping the size of the Pacific, I was overwhelmed by an awful lot of blue and printed coordinates of latitude, longitude, and sea depth. Our port of call destination, the Hawaiian Islands, was no more than a curved string of tiny, tan dots just below the Tropic of Cancer. Iconic island images came to mind such as palm trees, pineapples, bars, suntanned girls in swimsuits, volcanic peaks, Waikiki Beach, Mustang convertibles, and Diamond Head.

Perhaps one of the most disconcerting things about having such a cartographically oriented mind as I did occurred at sea. With no reference to land points, maps had less value; there was only water! As unexpectedly upsetting as this was to me, nobody else particularly cared. This is why

I took to watching stars and sunsets in attempts to recapture my innate sense of direction. There were only these perpetually repetitive breaking waves of water below the bow until one day when we began approaching "land ho" near dusk. Far, blue-green bumps silhouetted the western sky after days of tedious shades of blue; it was hypnotic.

The spell wore off as we slowly navigated shorelines rounding Big Island. After dinner, Oahu's volcanic peaks came into view. At this tropical latitude, days and nights differed only a couple minutes in length. I stretched my legs and looked at wafts of orange-yellow clouds like a deep yellow egg yolk sinking below the horizon. I walked along the starboard (right side facing the bow) handrail; the half-submerged sun cast a strikingly bright reflection line on water straight toward me until it finally succumbed to its nightly resting place. For geo-head me, this wasn't just an aesthetic canvas to savor, it was a useful place for contemplation!

I pondered this topographically, envisioning a global map and ships amid deep blue emptiness. Brooding over nautical possibilities in a way I could do, I concluded we must have been traveling southwest for this to occur since I was starboard (otherwise a sun would set left of bow).

This pondering lingered during the more than a day that it took to ever so slowly approach Oahu. Late the next day, it captured my attention so completely I skipped a shoot 'em up John Wayne movie below deck. Now turning north toward Honolulu itself, I visualized how one might guess direction just by looking at a setting sun (a bright idea!); and, though dangerous to human eyes, it was still intriguing to my piqued geographic attitude. I had an unquenched thirst for something more tangible.

Despite likely imprecision of any geographical conjectures I might have, it was a lot more entertaining than the movie might have been. It was a way to grasp spatial images and envisage a tapestry map of blue with a string of islands to differentiate this new ocean-based location from my landlocked desert upbringing.

On main deck there was a nighttime skyline and city lights mirrored in the harbor water. Skyscrapers and streams of auto taillights created moving red lines between the lights. I threaded plats and plans with highways and moving cars on my own internal cartographic backdrop.

My friends Phil (left), me with map, and John ready to tour.

Engaging as this image was over watching a gun-slinger movie (or, worse yet, polishing boots), Honolulu slowly closed in. I could detect traffic sounds from the shore. We eventually docked late after midnight.

The next day, more military gear and supplies were loaded onboard; docking was pretty much all military business except for tangible pangs of America we might see for the last time.

Half of us got a seven-hour pass to check out Honolulu; the other half got a pass the next day. Three of my friends and I rented a pink jeep and saw the sights on the Oahu beaches. I was in charge of the maps.

Direction Detection

After four days of further loading and touring around, our trio of ships departed Pearl Harbor. On the first day out to sea at Battalion muster, our A Company commanding officer, Captain Velasquez, described our trek toward Vietnam, giving an idea about how long it was going to take to get there as well as daily routines and agendas.

We were given lectures about tropical diseases, plants, animals, and insects. We were told we needed to keep hydrated. Other tropic topics dealing with food and hygiene occupied our attentions between taxing sessions of push-ups and running around top deck every day. But we had ample free time too.

After dinner, watching the sun approach horizon, I noted we were heading a bit right of the sun's reflection line back toward the ship. This struck me odd because I had already been hypothesizing how we'd now continue heading due west (i.e., straight into the sunset dead on) at a notably different angle from the one we traveled between San Diego and Hawaii. As my map head kicked in, something now didn't seem right.

On my way to quarters, by habit I paused at the bridge where that sprawling five-foot wide world map hung. Between San Diego and Hawaii, I counted lines of north-south longitude (time zones) and used these as measures of distance instead of daily-announced knots by the bridge captain. I was thus able to comprehend a combination of time and east-to-west distance traveled after becoming comfortable with this daily routine.

This time, instead of longitude, I zeroed in on latitudes (lines parallel to equator), particularly the Tropic of Cancer itself (23°+ degrees north). Then it hit me! Had we been sailing toward Vietnam, the sun *had* to set almost precisely due west. But the sun had not; it was setting portside left of bow.

Three weeks before, the summer solstice occurred as it does every June 21. My internal orientation process became preoccupied with this new mind map that was forming to fit the islands and countries in the Western Pacific from a new perspective. Though trivial to others, this became paramount to me.

I readied myself intellectually during dinner to explore the theory. I positioned myself amidships at sunset topside (topmost open deck). I scrutinized how the sun's now orange center kissed the horizon so I could determine deviation from due west. I was careful never to look directly into the sun.

The author spent a lot of time topdeck just before sunset.

Presuming handrails on both sides parallel to the ship's bow-to-stern midline, the outer edge of these rails became handy to use as a measuring reference since line of sight down the ship's side would be the same as its midline, indeed parallel to it to determine a precise course of travel. Thus, positioning myself amidships starboard or portside instead of at the bow (where a midline is hard to establish since side rails converge and are obviously not parallel), using the handrail to measure from enabled observing actual directional headings with remarkable, handcrafted precision once daily at sunset.

At summer's solstice, the sun is directly over the Tropic

of Cancer, the furthest north it travels with a perpendicular azimuth at midday, as well as setting precisely due west on June 21 if one were on that line of latitude. We were now a few degrees south of the Tropic of Cancer, and I knew the sun's zenith was heading south each night at about one degree every three days or so. We were also less than three weeks past the solstice, so the sun was almost directly overhead. Had we been going southwest toward Vietnam, the sun had to set starboard to the right of the bow's midline.

It wasn't.

We were *not* heading toward Vietnam; we were heading ever so slightly west by northwest! A feeling of intellectual stealth crept through me on this private non-John-Wayne type of quest. I audaciously turned another page in my mind map.

Using scratch paper with a directional 3 o'clock representing 90°, I could halve it to make 45° and halve it again to make 22½°, and yet again to make 11¼° then estimate a fairly precise course of travel in degrees using an assumption, of course, that the ships were traveling in a straight line daily. Using this method, I guesstimated we were heading 9° to 10° north of due west on a straight course just south of the Tropic of Cancer while accommodating the daily southbound sun. The ship's heading remained dead-on straight, west by northwest. I detected no change in course not even any yaw, pitch, or roll that might distort calculations. I wanted to validate presumptions more accurately then make a legitimate destination forecast.

The next day on the bridge after our mile run on top deck, I used a straight edge of my lined tablet paper with deviation in degrees penciled in from the night before. I plotted two extensions of direction onto the world map, keeping margins of error in mind. I extended these two imaginary 9° and 11° northwest straight lines so that projections headed from a start point (an estimated position three day's travel straight west by northwest of Honolulu) further west into the East China Sea.

This created a narrow east-to-west map triangle where our real intended destination must be within. I couldn't conceive any logical destination from the data, but I knew it definitely was *not* toward Vietnam at all. With two days' worth of calculations, I reported findings casually to my A Company commander, Captain Raymond Velasquez, thinking he might be interested in such conjectures.

"So where do you think we're headin', marine?" he asked me, smiling as officers unsurprisingly do sometimes with enlisted personnel. He was obviously entertained by my plausible theory but not yet wishing to summarily dismiss my logic or enthusiasm, as it was genuinely backed up by pencil and paper calculations. He was perhaps amused by the absurdity of its implications since he had been convinced we were heading to Vietnam himself, or maybe he was a little bored with the calmness of other onboard routines. I could tell he understood the word "azimuth" when he mentioned how tiny shadows were on the top deck at midday, almost nonexistent. However, his eyebrows were still raised in smiling doubt. This might be entertainment, but it was not science. (Or was it?)

"Of course I don't know exactly, sir, but according to calculations I can say we're definitely not heading toward Nam, that's for sure... even taking into account the customary passage around the Philippines." He declined to go with me to the wall map on the bridge, perhaps because he didn't want to be seen being *instructed* on something by a low-ranking, enlisted man.

The captain then said, "Well, maybe it's the curve of the earth." He smiled again, maybe wanting to exhibit some of his own knowledge despite a contrived voice. What he didn't know was that in a fairly straight east-west line, curvature makes little difference at this tropical latitude. I supposed for a moment he was talking about earth's curved surface to joke with me. After all, maybe he was thinking how airline routes look bowed in northern latitudes and distorted on "flattened out" Mercator-type map projections even though straight, but it's not as true in the tropics and irrelevant for this explanation.

I knew getting into technical explanations might go over his head, so I respectfully asked him, if I came up with target destinations, if he'd check the bridge for accuracy. Captain Velasquez said he would with a semi-honest captainesque smile. We talked more about why shadows cast on deck around midday were so small. It was gratifying to have discussions like this.

Pinpointing Possibilities

The next afternoon I reverified pencil calculations,

reapplying a 9° to 11° estimate to two straight lines on paper positioned on the bridge's Mercator map projection. This created a narrow margin within which I extended my paper further until it reached the coast of mainland China a second time, re-creating my 9°-11° triangle.

The triangle width wasn't *that* narrow by the time it reached China, but it didn't produce any obvious destinations either. I scrutinized the triangle thoroughly for clues; surely we were not heading toward communist China! With squinting precision and speculating likely options, I approached Captain V again, offering direction, degrees, and endpoints within a narrow triangular band of choices.

"Okinawa or maybe the island of Iwo Jima seem most likely," I announced with academic confidence, "maybe Wake Island or even one of the uninhabited islands north of Guam in the Marianas; theoretically, even Taiwan."

There was logic guessing Okinawa inasmuch it was a naval base, but it was a bit outside my margin of error, as was Wake. Iwo Jima had little more than a historical significance in World War II for marines but there was no strategic reason to go there since it was largely uninhabited. But the island was in my triangle.

I decided to speculate and said to the captain, "If I were to choose, I'd say we're heading for Iwo Jima." My mind thought about our companion ship, named Iwo Jima, sailing parallel to us a half mile north while feeling like TV attorney Perry Mason in court, announcing findings of evidence. I didn't flinch.

"So *that's* what you think, eh?" The captain nodded again with the same raised-eyebrow smile, but as promised, he later checked in with his navy friend on the bridge. Meanwhile, I reverified the ship's direction after dinner at sunset for the third day in a row; I detected no changes. I didn't meet Captain V again right away, but when I did he was more straight-faced; I took this more as an academic compliment among business associates, but not necessarily within our military environment. He related his bridge chat with a professor-like stare.

"You know, Choc, I'm not sure I communicated your angles or degrees accurately, but I do think I explained your premise and logic." Captain Velasquez talked to me more like an intellectual colleague or peer than the PFC I was. Captain V went on to explain how we were indeed heading for Vietnam . . . eventually. And, he revealed to me how we were going to go to the Philippines first . . . a confidential detour I did *not* know. Still, right now he didn't know our true interim destination for sure, nor had he thought to believe anything beyond what all other officers presumed to be factual.

Captain V addressed me in an unusual but considerate voice, "The bridge officer confirmed sailing from Hawaii, both Vietnam as well as the Philippines were similar in direction." After a pause, choosing words cautiously, he went on, "But the lieutenant on duty said our interim destination was classified and on a need-to-know basis. I'd have to confer with the battalion commander or ship's captain for details."

Captain Velasquez wasn't troubled, but he was revealing a fascinating manner. He didn't say so, but he appreciated learning things of value from *inside* his company. Without pressing naval officers for disclosure of classified information, Velasquez said he intended to ask the destination in question tomorrow at officers' mess since he sat with the colonel regularly. Although the captain was expressing appreciation for this pending discovery, it wasn't particularly consequential information. What it did give him was an edge of knowledge no one else among his military peers had, and he was using it. I got the impression he was more typically on the receiving side of information; this "intelligence" thus had value.

Later, Captain V told me the battalion commander admitted we were indeed heading for Iwo Jima after describing with an insider's smile the difficulty he had prying it out of the colonel. The captain also revealed mentioning my calculations and paperwork. Despite pride of achievement for such a trivial matter, I couldn't dismiss the feeling Captain V was probably taking most of the credit, but I never found that out. I did receive more than one interesting acknowledgment from other A Company lieutenants when this story was privately retold to me later on. Lieutenant Innspruker told me, "Did you ever consider becoming an officer? …least that's what Captain thinks …we need guys like you."

My respect for Captain V lifted for extending some credit to me no matter how much or how little. It was after all, an exceedingly inconsequential point of fact, but I felt exceptionally gratified for its discovery prior to the event itself.

I never heard reference to this again, but a few did have a sense for my conscientiousness about maps; that pleased me too. My own enlisted ego was inflated since I got it right without any technical instruments, and I felt pretty good about adjusting my geographic acclimation to the vast ocean expanse in this way.

I reconjure this picture again and again every time I hear the words "parallel lines." I weighed the personal value of this labor of love and its worthiness versus its actual insignificance and concluded that what I gained was fulfillment for doing something no one else had thought to do. True or not, that alone was sufficient to produce "A+" feelings.

Despite disclosure to selected officers, Captain V admonished me to "keep the secret for a very special event yet to come." Of course I agreed.

Attention!

A few days later and an hour before the entourage of three parallel ships approached the island of Iwo Jima the morning of July 24, starboard side, we were briefly updated about the history, personal sacrifices, and strategic consequences of this particular consequential Second World War battle. The Corps was especially significant because of the many hundreds of marines who perished upon this uninhabited Pacific pockmark of desolate blue-gray slopes.

Promptly on cue, every single marine assembled on top deck and stood at attention for over one full hour.

Ships' engines had been cut and there was utter silence. Only the flapping, snapping American flags and marine standards posted above us could be heard as we noiselessly drifted past Iwo Jima without even any swish in the water. Everyone reverently stared at the island as we remained at full, rigid attention eyeing the historic island slowly edging left to right, passing right in front of us.

Finally, everyone saluted on command and held angled right arms in place for several minutes as ships' engines spewed groans and regained modest, westbound, ten-knot speed. A sacred event similar to communion (without red wine) occurred on all three ships solemnly and simultaneously.

Once our internal amens were relieved, a second "attention" was followed by a prompt "dismissed" just before we dispersed slowly and respectfully off deck. A few whispered, "Semper fi's" were somberly exchanged.

Very little else interrupted the afternoon sun while this small but historically prominent symbol of Second World War sacrifice eventually disappeared from view to our right as the island picked up hints of solar orange for those who chose to linger and ponder this eastward reflection.

Naturally, I noted the setting sun that evening and how it had finally shifted significantly further starboard, setting at about 45° to midline on main deck as we veered southwest toward Subic Bay, Philippines. I needed no paper drawings to identify exactly our real destination or direction, but of course, each evening after chow I observed my orangey cohort, and the now more dignified swishing of ocean water streaming alongside ship.

I lingered just a little longer than most others, not so much for extended respect for those marines who had fallen so heroically, but the improbability for my being there to see it at all. My self-esteem gained something for the uniqueness of my predictive actions that week. My soul was privately assuaged that I was honestly one of them on the same team . . . this skinny wimp had value after all.

I eyed the expansive wall map on the bridge every evening, and I proved once again to myself how well maps portray their purpose and about how well I spoke their language.

6

Filipino Breather

July 1966

In Subic Bay, we loaded more gear during the day. Free time in the little made-for-military local town of Olangapo brought late nights, cheap booze, sticky women, and hangovers. I lost $25 to a pickpocket's clever hand and learned not to walk alone. I never did taste any monkey meat on bamboo skewers, and I avoided stepping off wet curbs into sewer water trickling between gooey cobblestone channels.

Two days after departing Subic Bay, the battalion held a practice "landing" where we plodded ashore after pounding up and down on surf and thudded onto sand in this first wave as a practice run using naval landing craft (we called them "Mike" boats). In a few days it would be a real landing where a real enemy might be waiting for us.

But now we moved inland for a week of dense jungle training on the island of Mindoro, getting sweaty and muddy, warding off nasty crawly bugs and creeping critters, and resolving how to manage jungle rot from

Seated left to right: Local Filipino photographer, Tom Soda, Lonnie Siebrandt, me, and John Bierne at a local bar in the town of Olangapo near Subic Bay in the Philippines.

trudging in wet boots eighteen hours a day often in heavy rain. As green fatigues turned orangey-brown, our sweat made orangey-brown paste on our faces as well. But we ate our meals, kept rifles oiled, and made do with mutual misery.

Other than that, the countryside was lushly green, fertile, and the people were friendly for those who noticed. Only our guides could speak Tagalog, so there was little communication with locals.

Except for infected feet, we departed the Philippines feeling like world travelers with stories to tell. It took a few showers and a thorough drying out to get our street sense back in synch with normalcy. Despite peeling skin and red polka-dotted rashes in all sorts of sunshineless places, a few days remained for healing as our ships proceeded to chaperone us toward the ultimate destination.

7

Another Normandy

August-September 1966

After a week of Filipino-styled prep and southbound sailing, we went "in-country" i.e., inland into Vietnam itself not far from Saigon in a place called Vung Tàu. Now an amphibious assault team, four platoons of the twenty-sixth, as well as platoons from the other ships, landed just as they had at Omaha Beach in France during World War II using Mike boats.

Bottom hinged doors banged down so olive-green throngs could jump into about two feet of water. The big difference between here and Normandy was no immediate return fire even though a few were spooked into discharging weapons into morning mist amid shadowy darkness and strange, curly manifestations hanging from trees.

I remained onboard the Vancouver with Captain V for the first excursion and listened to radio transmissions and squawking panicky voices, waiting for cues when the second wave would launch for going ashore. The next day, I accompanied Captain ashore. Though anxieties elevated, nothing much happened. After several days sailing north combined with a second stop in the Philippines, we approached a beach near the DMZ (demilitarized zone) in Quang Tri Province. Another Normandy-type landing occurred again. But this time our first wave hit resistence. We heard repetitious rata-tat-tatting of machine gunfire amidst terrified lieutenants on captain's radio aboard ship. Within seconds, rockets exploded as jets flew close overhead and dropped explosives a few hundred feet from open radio mikes. We heard quivering voices followed by excruciating seconds of silence. Anxious voices slowly relived static details.

After things settled down, helicopters carried WIAs (injured soldiers), KIAs (killed in action), and other staff back to ships. I accompanied Captain V by chopper to the Iwo to interview wounded and review KIAs. One long row of our A Company were dead and laid out on harbor deck uncovered, face up.

I stared at Lt. Inspruker's open mouth. His blond hair was streaked brownish red, but his body was intact. The next marine in line looked asleep, but when I passed his lifeless corpse, half his head was cleanly missing with an empty pinkish-gray brain cavity neatly exposed and visible only from the other side. Half-naked others had red dots here and there where bullets pierced torsoes with less blood than what I may have imagined, maybe because of rain or maybe because they'd already been cleaned up, I didn't know. Other battalion losses were similarly arranged in neat rows, company by company (maybe twenty for the entire battalion), with each row of bodies encircled by us few stewards witnessing and recording the final event.

The impact of death itself disrupted my thinking: the orderly care and arrangement of bodies; tender handling of arms and legs still limber (rigor mortis not yet set); chaplains bowing over each, pausing with moving lips; gentle lifting of personal items like dog tags, rosaries, crosses, and pocket bibles; numerous small but consequential tangibles like wrinkled letters and lucky coins; trash, like broken cookies, matches and cigarettes, ball point pens and Chapstick all amid wafting pungent antiseptic smells, all witnessed by well-hidden tears and solemnness.

Within less than ninety minutes, all KIAs were zippered into long, dark green, heavy plastic bags for imminent transport off ship. Their belongings were collected into smaller plastic bags with identifying tags; a couple of us from A Company gathered ours for transport back to the Vancouver.

A thickness of recollections clogged my head as live images evaporated, transforming human forms into hard inanimate objects. The fragility of life manifested itself into something unpredictably natural but untimely, anticipated yet random, logical but wrong.

Second Wave

For a couple days, there was no field action. Then Captain V and I flew by helicopter to join still-remaining, already-entrenched A Company marines. Midmorning, sticky insects were scouting out breakfast (me) as I carried radio for the captain; sweat made my clothes tacky but tasty for them. That I couldn't scrape my back under the radio was a tedious itching annoyance, but once we set up headquarters camp I scratched. All conversations dealt with the first wave's ordeals and injuries.

One of the choppers readied to leave the Vancouver for the Iwo.

This time, platoons went out with frowns, squinting eyes, and ready-to-fire rifles. However, they came back empty-handed. Nothing. There was silence except for occasional gunfire from our own weapons. The air was laden with strange, almost pepper-spicy aromas. Silence. In less than a week, Captain Velasquez concluded "Charlie," our Viet Cong opponents, had taken off; so we returned to the Vancouver with little else to report.

Unexpectedly, it became my task to scrutinize all the KIA's personal effects, looking at articles that had been already removed from their bodies as well as examining their possessions stowed onboard ship. I was to carefully throw away items that wouldn't be sent home like off-color photographs and drawings, inappropriate correspondence (I scanned all letters and notes inside wallets, pocket bibles, and other hiding places), cigarettes, marijuana, and so on.

At first, I lingered on words the dead marine had written down, studying handwriting that would never pen another letter. Then there were family or girlfriends' smiles on wrinkled photographs; they were daily reminders about those who cared. All symbols of military preparation from bibles to chevrons sewn on shirts not yet worn, from decks of cards to lucky charms all became poignant.

Studying letters received in the two or three weeks that followed became the most moving task as I read recountings of home events, and cautions of hope and pride.

Troubling at first, I eventually justified these invasive acts into the privacy of other individuals who could no longer object to my forays into their souls. The respect I crafted was based upon mutuality . . . how I'd want to be similarly treated had roles been reversed.

Later, I typed condolence letters to next of kin for Captain V to sign. These were standard letters with a few phrases injected to personalize the message in addition to names and places. Then I updated admin records, kept track of troop strength data, and reported it to headquarters daily in order to assure replacement troops were promptly and appropriately reassigned.

This had been my introduction in-country.

Disembarkation

Onboard Vancouver we headed north for Da Nang, but sunsets over thin-shaded shores were dull. Dark, green jungle coastlines became a new repetitive reference outline for my mind, a skinny white beach with few distinguishing characteristics mile after mile with occasional fishermen casting nets from boats and black preying raptors bucking breezes to seize upon what the nets might discard.

I kept track of angled proximities toward shore; this map-head of mine was thus fed and oriented nonetheless. We headed north by northeast in shallower gray water by day, cloud-covered skies at night. Swishing water reflected flashing glances from the moon. These covert acts of consolation were intellectually useful, but I made no new worthy geographical-type discoveries.

Shoreline near Da Nang from onboard just before porting.

It was nearly impossible to get in touch with Steve who'd been stationed near Da Nang; and, we didn't meet up for months. We communicated by mail even though we were no more than maybe twenty miles apart.

On board I made a new friend, Jim Logan, who always had something to say that would make me laugh and taught me not to take myself too seriously. "You're a lot smarter than you look, but in your case, you'd hafta be," he'd jest with me. I needed this kind of balance. Jim would later become my best man, and remains my longest-lasting friend to this day.

I mused about afternoon daylight right here along the coast of Vietnam as only I could do; it was the middle of the night back home in New Mexico. Those twenty-four time zones around the globe were all numbered; Albuquerque was twelve away.

This was a new place. My mind loitered, waiting for a next trek as I conjured thoughts of old friends at home walking upside-down. Without such mind-dawdling, indefinable tensions, anxieties of *nothingness* would surface . . . things I've found hard to manage unless some form of imagination took over.

Lines of *longitude* and time zones are not so hard to understand, nor is the Tropic of Cancer or any of the other *latitudes*. It's a way to think about things like coastlines, setting suns, and parallel lines. It's another way to get from here to there, no matter where *there* might happen be.

Once approaching the *there*, a person like me needs to get a new ticket, the *next* ticket to places where no maps were yet in my head.

8

Pings

Winter 1966

There must be libraries of war stories out there. After all, those who participated remember many events so vividly they're embedded in their heads like cement. But brushes with severe adversity, near-death events, or gut-wrenching surprises are more than just exciting memories or another book on the shelf; they're dents in our own impenetrable armor, scars on our souls, and eventually wrinkles on our face. Some remain resolute reminders of old private wounds.

Yet for those who waded through such waters (or in this case, rice paddies), they explain much as well. There are countless military events no one remembers at all no matter what, but there's also a definable value for what particular incidents turn out to mean, an appreciated value that comes along . . . way after uniforms no longer fit, like those chevron-studded life souvenirs stowed away in the closet or attic for good.

I had my share of experiences but admittedly far fewer than most other grunts because my duties led down different paths. Company commander, Captain Velasquez, who I came to respect as a smart and well-educated man, sought Vietnam as a personal mission. He had a brother who either died or sustained injury; perhaps he wanted to assuage or avenge a despicable act or display that intention. However, as a thoughtful but not overly aggressive man, this academic captain was not a ground-pounding athletic-type marine either. He never liked getting hands dirty or feet wet.

From a privileged and trusted position, I overheard the captain's revealing remarks with others in charge, words not meant for those hunkered down in bunkers to hear. As he seldom left home base unless he had to, I grew to appreciate it since it meant I didn't either. Not being an emblematic ground-pounding marine myself, I thus avoided some pretty nasty stuff!

I did have several distinctive assignments that developed into less common purposes without any marine team limelights or *Stars and Stripes* headlines. No, these weren't badge-worthy or otherwise documentable, just some unique experiences not recorded or written down by anyone else.

Having attended Vietnamese language school, I could translate things like propaganda flyers that were scattered about; but honestly, my translations weren't particularly useful. Most of these were printed by the United States for consumption by the locals anyway. These leaflets dealt mostly with pro-American or anti-Viet Cong messages.

A typical propaganda flyer encouraging trust for American troops.

Occasionally there was a printed sign or local newspaper, but these were interesting, not tactical. My knack for languages ended up being of greater value to me over later years than ever during the war effort.

Besides typing official correspondence, another task was carrying the captain's radio on my back whenever we exited the perimeter, admittedly not often. They issued a shotgun for me to use "just in case" for captain's protection, which to my dismay seemed to rust overnight until those plastic M-16s came along, which were more practical for everyone including me. I never test-fired that shotgun, and only carried four shotgun shells in case I ever needed them.

My first seven months were spent at a place called Hill 55, a plateau of nonagricultural land suitable for military-type operations. Now, most called it "Hill Five-Five," not "Hill Fifty-five," which distinguished those who worked there from visitors or "just-landeds" (i.e., newbies).

Hill 55 was a few hours' drive southwest from Da Nang. Headline-worthy news events seemed to be going on elsewhere. It's not that nothing happened near Hill 55, but nothing aggressively menacing happened on a regular basis. We heard stories of other "real bad" places, and though Hill 55 was not a very nice place, it was a *better* place to be than so many others.

The most gruesome stories around Hill 55 dealt with guys stepping on poisonous punji sticks or leftover mines from earlier French interactions with enemies from the north. Some got shot at in jeeps and on patrol, or picked off by isolated snipers one at a time. It was bad enough to be sure, but we slept inside screen-sided shelters and walked around camp with some watchful nonchalance and neverending respect for hostile opposition. We'd witness injured marines airlifted by chopper to Da Nang. We'd see bloodstains, hear rat-ta-tat-tat gunfire in the distance, and helicopter noise. There was always more "over there." We slept at night interrupted only by perimeter watches (9:00 to 12:00 PM, 12:00 to 3:00 AM, or 3:00 to 6:00 AM) where little ever happened.

Officers wearing shiny birds or stars on their lapels or journalists in their brand new, starched olive drab "fatigues" (to make them look authentic?) visited us. We got haircuts from villagers who set up makeshift huts outside our perimeter. These villagers gratefully took the red-colored military currency (military script, or MPCs) we had to use while in-country instead of greenbacks or local piasters. American commerce was genuinely welcomed and probably needed by nearby inhabitants.

The author showing off his new rifle.

Later on in March at Hill 55, they exchanged our rifles for new M-16s, a rather plasticized version of our old M-14s. M-16s are technically much more advanced but harder to keep clean. They malfunctioned more frequently, especially if you were not thorough with your cleaning process. We were given the opportunity to test fire these new weapons and they appeared to work fine to me. Most people just became so intimate with their own rifle it was challenging to make the switch. This was a very common subject of conversation at chow or while on watch.

Unique ways to keep clean.

One time, sexy Hollywood movie actress Jayne Mansfield came to Hill 55 so we all could take photographs of her. A few of us took photographs *with* her. She probably spoke four or five sentences, put her arm around a few of us, and did little else beyond smiling at the camera while she raised her bare knee to rub our belt buckles. There were lots and lots of camera flashes. This occurred mere months before she died in a brutal car accident in Mississippi.

While Hill 55 was no paradise, we did have privileges. We had time to read the *Stars and Stripes*, the made-for-military newspaper distributed in Nam to catch up on all the latest edited-for-troops news. The beer was typically barely cool (never cold). The mail came regularly. Attitudes and demeanors reflected seriousness without signs of panic. While our at-sea operations were called Deckhouse II and Deckhouse III, there were many other names for these in-country operations (e.g., Pawnee, Shasta, Independence, Crickett, Ardmore, etc. ...too many to remember). These were referenced here or there in the Stars and Stripes starting in August 1966. Strategically, we were important; most of us were just unsure exactly how.

Maybe this was partly another reason Hill 55 was so popular with celebrities and journalists; it was an accessible place to go to that was in the middle of everything going on in Vietnam... not where high-risk deadly events actually *were* happening, just where they *could be* happening.

One time renowned author, John Steinbeck, came to visit us on the Hill. While it was an informal visit where he told us about all good things American, he was surrounded by colonels, newspaper guys, and photographers who wanted to be seen *with* him.

But Hill 55 was convenient for us marines too. Some of us rode courier jeeps back to Da Nang usually to pick up or drop off someone who couldn't get on a chopper, but it also allowed one or two of us "to get outta Dodge" and away from the often boring daily routines of Hill 55.

If we were lucky, we'd spend a couple of hours at sunny China Beach to work on suntans and stories, both envied by everyone else at the mess hall later while downing our high protein, potatoes, and one green vegetable dinners. I was able to go to China Beach twice.

Marines on Hill 55, five miles southwest of Da Nang, give first-hand information to author John Steinbeck on the Vietnamese war. Steinbeck (center foreground) holds an M-79 grenade launcher.

John Steinbeck (center) telling us some of his stories.

During this time I learned about R&R. Unsure what this acronym actually meant, I thought it stood for rest and relaxation (some thought it meant rest and recreation).

Marines became eligible to go once they were in country for four to six months. Of a half dozen exotic destinations, I chose Hong Kong and the opportunity surfaced in December. For five days I toured the streets, ate at one fancy floating restaurant in the harbor, checked out abundant hot nightclubs, marveled at New Year's Eve celebrations, had a hand-tailored sports coat fitted precisely to my specs (I mailed it home), and then flew back to my day job.

Paddy Plodding

While packing up and trudging off into the bush were regular events, it wasn't often for me personally, maybe once every ten days or two weeks . . . unlike other grunts who'd head out four or five times a week. Some were overnighters where we'd entertain an audience of insects amid humid, sweaty patrols below canopies of leaves . . . without flashlights, limelights, or applause. While these performances could be repetitive and boring, without warning there were those one or two forays in ten where snipers, camo'ed in foliage offstage, would make their mark. Or maybe one of us would step on a nasty jagged punji stick. Most times though, Charlie never waited around for the credits despite a stealthy returned-fire encore. Those bugs seemed to know; they took off whenever rifles were fired.

One day, Captain V announced he was going on an all-day patrol, an event that needed preparation since usually one of his lieutenants led these. The next morning exiting through checkpoints at the perimeter, a dozen or more of us zigzagged around unfenced fields as darkness fogged into a subdued dawn. Right behind the captain, I was last in line with a radio and my new M-16.

Once we determined our direction, we spoke little. As first in line, Corporal Sanders had "point" and knew exactly where the captain wanted him to go. With the lieutenant in the middle, we walked purposefully yet cautiously cognizant of unwelcome surprises. The patrol didn't otherwise *do* much, going up a rise, down through brush, and splashing into mud. We used few military tactics other than trying to eyeball what we never could see.

I was present when the captain radioed S-2 (battalion intelligence) while sharing well-folded topographical maps with Sanders and his lieutenant; they always talked privately just above a whisper as if someone might listen. I could read, "topo sheets" better than most, so I followed along ably with my ears and understood coordinates to pinpoint positions or request airstrikes or mortar drops if necessary. While not knowing our actual mission or why we chose the routes we did, I at least appreciated the where of it all.

Our boots did a good job keeping feet dry in the morning. We ate C-rats (C-rations) for lunch and drank water from canteens whenever we felt the urge as we sloshed through paddies. We lost site of the Hill amidst jungle foliage in between farmers' planted beds. Humid air hung hot, heavy, and quiet, so we sweated profusely as our necks turned red.

Today's "job" seemed pointless; the captain wasn't saying much, and we weren't seeing much or doing much except making repetitious zigzags around paddies for miles. The only sounds were slurping soles, slugging mud, and occasional bird twills.

Often Captain V paused to use the radio I carried in a knapsack. Whenever this occurred, I faced away from him as he used the backpack like a telephone booth, or we'd sit on the ground back to back. This made calls appear more confidential. In this position I scrutinized back where we had just traversed. Anyone viewing us from a distance could easily surmise who the patrol leader probably was by observing who carried the radio, a disconcerting thought.

He calculated two, six digit numerical coordinates from topo sheets to pinpoint various positions for S-2 back on 5-5. However, Velasquez virtually had no information to report. From time to time, I thought he reported suspicions rather than facts since I saw what he saw, but it kept us all a little more sensitive than we might otherwise have been. The trip did have some practice value after all.

Our boots became muddier as the day went on. Shirts shined dark green from sweat, staining floury white as they dried. Our palms were slick, sometimes slippery. Surely I wasn't the only one wondering about the point of the exercise, but the captain was taking it seriously, so we did too.

The front end of the patrol began ascending above the paddy when something happened.

Encounter

Thick humidity-laden air muffled noises, but the next sounds were unmistakable.

Ping! Ping! There were maybe five fairly light, popping *ping* sounds. I saw splashes off to my left in the paddy water, incoming gunfire! My knees buckled instinctively as I splayed into a prone position, rolling into the paddy itself with a thorough thump-splat. Everyone in front leaped over top of the rise, taking cover. I glimpsed with blurred vision how Captain V ground-rolled then crawled over the last couple feet just like we used to practice in boot camp.

Although I carried our patrol's means of communication on my back, I'm not sure this actually occurred to me at that very moment. However, at least the radio was dry.

By the end of the no more than five seconds this all took, I had fallen flat into water face down. I had one closed eye underwater, my nostrils were just barely above waterline to breathe, and my heart pounded. I heaved quietly but forcibly gasped air, trying not to make movements anywhere else in my body. I swallowed some brown paddy water and then coughed, shaking in fear. My face looked right and slightly ahead; the pings had come from my left and behind. I listened intently with my one above-water ear, shifting nothing else but my nose.

Not being able to see anyone in my restrained state of panic, I didn't know what to do next except not to move.

It was oddly quiet and I trembled, but my one-ear hearing was acute. Two more popping pings crackled in my above-water ear from not sure where, but close enough to hear pops and water splashes. My gut shuddered.

Even though I had a mouth full of paddy water residue I couldn't spit out, I felt a bit protected lying in these tepid liquids. I knew my body might be shielded by lying low in four-inch deep opaque paddy spittle. Shivering as if cold in the heavy heat of afternoon sun, I detected my rifle barrel was still above water, but the trigger was below; would it still fire?

Franticly listening for cues to use from one above-water ear, I felt every muscle and vein tighten, even my carotids, as blood furiously pushed through my neck. Inconspicuousness was top priority. Trying to yell but unable, I spit out some brown paste from my mouth, striving not to shift my head or let any more paddy gunk flow in.

Suddenly feeling alone, I needed a clear head to think; I didn't want to react impetuously. Not thinking straight, I presumed for a moment I might be wounded. There was no blood or pain amidst the grit as I contracted muscles and bones to check further. I *could* detect heartbeats in my chest and my neck almost audibly.

But everything else was mysteriously quiet. Sweat dripped through my above-water eye and blurred my vision, causing me to keep blinking to avoid salty stings. Yet, I felt a cool metallic rod of panic emanating from my upper spine, perhaps an unconscious spur to do something other than slurp gravel or just grovel inside my predicaments.

I withheld shivers, thinking they may somehow be seen. I wondered where the others were. Were they hit? Did they rush on to get out of there? There were no sounds. Maybe I *was* hurt but without pain. Did they leave without me? I began to sort my thoughts and make plans; my mind readied but nothing materialized beyond lifting my left nostril above the water line that shifted my head slightly up. I could now also see hazy clouds in the sky, little else except for itsy bitsy wet shoots of brackish green two inches away. Rice?

But despite an absence of sound, my rigid brain swooned as my subconscious command post took over.

Time crawled along as my neck veins continued to thump rhythmically. Why was my vision blurry? I jerked my head against water trickling back into my left nostril with a twitching jolt. I gazed down at my body, detecting dampness seeping horizontally into my boots *and* up my leg as water soaked in. I felt no pain and I looked to see if I could see anything red, but I didn't. Again, after moving each limb and joint to assure nothing was broken or injured, I took a deep breath and exhaled sluggishly and cleared passageways with guttural coughs and spits. Even though I could detect slow motion heartbeats, I completely lost grip of time.

I struggled to think and choose a course of action. Several feet beyond my boots, I perceived something sticking straight up in the paddy water, like dark brown popsicle sticks. I focused as best I could on . . . stems of my glasses! I could not reach them. Only then did I fully comprehend why my eyesight had been fuzzy.

Fearing that my moving body would become a target, I pondered a next move while restraining involuntary panic. My presence of mind was only now coming to. Should I yell? Jump up and run? I concluded I might already look like a dead body. Was it good if I no longer looked like a target or body if nobody noticed? I slowly slouched my personal corpse sideways, reducing the height of the radio on my back but not wanting it to go underwater either. The radio could be a shield; it faced the direction of fire. The radio was pushing me down into the paddy water; why was it suddenly heavy?

Ping! Ping! Ping! Three more popping plops patted the paddy, near enough to break silence but not close enough to do damage. After ejecting more oral sludge, I tensed my arm and leg muscles which just made my motionless body tremble more. If I stood up and ran, I'd become an instant bullseye. My panicky mind conjectured the sniper must be looking right at me, but I couldn't see anything far away at all. Yet I couldn't just stay there and rot either.

Silence returned. Maybe the *radio* was the target. Dizzy with options, I remained quirkily serene in trance-like calm, even if it were a form of blind tranquility.

Fight back! Another couple of heartbeats throbbed for attention.

Just Do It!

The most disconcerting thing was that I could not rationally decide; my muddied mind solidified like concrete. Should I go back ten feet for my glasses or make a mad dash for the rise two body lengths in front of me? Should I ditch the weighty radio? There was an austere but admittedly temporary comfort just lying still since there were no aches or stings or blood. Mulling the now-warmed wetness moving up my thigh into my crotch, I remained thankful for those inches of pathway ledge dirt protecting me. Silence and isolation competed with conspicuousness and urgency.

Another single heartbeat, and then—

"Hey Choc, you okay?" came an invisible, very muffled but familiar voice from over the sandy rise. I could see no one; was it Sanders' voice? Trying to answer, water dribbled into my throat, I couldn't reply, nodding my head instead. But could they see me?

"Listen up! Can you hear me? Can . . . you . . . *hear* . . . me?"

The demand request was repeated in a stern, staggered voice, pausing between each word. I nodded again gurgling, and then lifted one hand barely out of the water to give a positive signal.

"Are you okay? Are you hurt? Can you get over on your own?" His voice turned rapid fire, demanding. "Now! I need to know *now*!"

"Yup!" My bubbling voice babbled, "Yuff," accompanied by a cough and throaty gurgle.

"On three, it's open fire, Choc! Yes, you! Listen up! Get up fast and roll your ass up and over the ridge. Can you do that? Can . . . you . . . *do* . . . that?"

"Yeah," I said, raising my head and clearing my throat, "Yes!" I called, spitting.

"Get ready!" advanced a different barely audible voice.

"Three . . . two . . . one," and then a quick-tempered barrage of gunfire commenced. Lumbering up with strength I didn't realize I could muster, I yanked my gut and rolled over twice as water sloshed from my helmet onto my shoulders, a surprisingly cool sensation as isolated tensions gave way. One strong arm snatched my shoulder sleeve and another arm pulled my collar, collectively heaving me through the spin with a radio still on my back. Everyone was hunkered down low on his knees.

The captain grabbed the mike and called in coordinates. He reported the incident in a subdued, matter-of-fact, almost whispered tone while Sanders grabbed my rifle and inspected me for wounds as I lay crouched but safe. During these very few seconds, I told him I wasn't hurt. Gunfire halted; then the captain concluded his call without saying anything; everyone else prepared to move out.

I mentioned my glasses, but no one thought it a good idea to go back even though there were no further pings. We finally stood hunched over and trod a low-postured trot away for the rest of our trek back to Hill 55 through jungle underbrush.

The captain's request for artillery backup had been recognized but denied even though coordinates were given. I did have my M-16 but couldn't see to shoot anything anyway. Feet sloshed inside boots. Although I didn't feel alone or isolated anymore, I still felt my belly muscles shake. No one was hurt. It was a nonevent. It didn't warrant weapon support from the Hill, troops, nor backup. It would be forgotten in a day. I learned later this whole episode of my lying in the paddy took less than just a couple minutes, two or maybe three, but there was an irreconcilable, ironed-on full hour of mental anguish in my recollection embedded in my subconsciousness.

The sandy hill had been blocking voices. Everyone had presumed I was hit, maybe dead, when his muffled calls went unanswered. I may have lain there alone that three-minute-long hour, but probably my brain speed had somehow decelerated to slow-mo. Coughing up more brown stuff, and bleary-eyed, I trudged back to Five-Five with the others; the wet radio still worked fine.

There are ample war stories. Blood, bodies blown apart, and savagery are all part of war and we remember these intense things to be sure. Amidst hours or days or weeks of boring, utterly nothing-to-report events, there are brief, indeed private moments where we gain introspection no matter heartbeat speed or circumstance. This wasn't a tale of gore or strategic troop movements. Nobody brought a camera to take pictures, but there was a thread of life fabric that became tangibly visible, maybe a strand or just a bit of fiber theretofore unrecognized. I understood its delicacy for what it was.

It was less a matter of life and death than it was like wearing a fragile, almost invisible cloak of self-preservation, bearing skin of self-awareness and intuition. A separate part of the brain was in instant reactive charge. We had barely considered the consequences of more than a minute or two ahead; only consequences of the next few seconds captured the entire soul instinctively in a form of personal, yet almost animalistic frenzy. It was a subconscientious reaction and an abandon of intellect. There were none of those recruiting poster images of intended visceral strength or confident prowess. No, the life and death of it all came long afterward in fleeting recollections, nightmares, and recurring dreams. Wrinkles creased the face even later.

In reality, this entire event was really, absolutely, nothing at all.

Yet, thinking back, it was a damned good thing I had a second pair of glasses.

9

Changing of the Guard

Winter 1967

Two weeks later, Captain V moved to S-2, the battalion's intelligence unit. He never went on another patrol, and I guess he was pretty happy about that. One of Velasquez's lieutenants, First Lt. Norman B. Centers, took the captain's place. Very few first lieutenants had ever been specifically appointed CO (company commander); it was an honor. Usually lieutenants inherited the job.

Norman Centers was a very strange man. He'd been a British marine but resigned to come to Nam via other military missions. An extraordinarily unhandsome man, balding, oversized lips, and a huge purple-stain birthmark covering half his face vertically, he was now in his mid-30s, war-weathered, looking rough and talking tough. His skinniness commanded attention when he walked. He had a lithe sense of humor and spoke well-pronounced, educated English without the "British accent" one might expect. Nobody messed with Stormin' Norman, no matter what . . . *nobody!* Centers liked being in A Company. After all, A was first and he always wanted to be first into the fray.

My compatriot in the HQ tent, Corporal Bierne, a postcard muscled marine, didn't mind the idea of going into the bush, so Centers picked him to carry radio (perhaps I looked too wimpy so I stayed behind). Stormin' patrolled often to keep an eye on things. I couldn't help noting how other officers admired him or avoided him and how well-respected he was. He breathed fire (at least I thought he did). Even gooks could see him coming (at least I thought they did) because Norman always complained "other lieutenants get to confront VC more often than I do." He didn't like "nothing to report" reports.

The word "gook" might have been a semi-derogatory term for Viet Cong, but we all commonly used either it or V.C. or "Charlie" for the Viet Cong. Stormin' liked to hiss the word *gooks* between his crooked teeth. I guess he thought it funny; *his* lieutenants dutifully chuckled.

During this time, Centers somehow persuaded our battalion navy doctor to operate cutting out a hefty quarter inch of lip tissue to improve his looks. Doc sliced horizontally across both lips, removed tissue, and then sewed incisions with stitches one morning. Centers went out on patrol the next day. After two weeks, it was surprising how well lips healed; his appearance improved a bit. Still, that massive birthmark scared most of us.

We conspicuously and dutifully said "sir" to Lt. Centers a lot more than required. He thrived on the word and thrived in his role.

10

Forced Landing

March 1967

Good fortune brought me a second R&R in Honolulu. In a full stint, marines received one R&R, occasionally two. I received two only because the person who put in for it was wounded and the slot would have been forfeited had I not taken his place. Such reprieves took one's mind off nasty things; Honolulu pulls it off with sunburn, everyone speaking English, rush-hour traffic, fast-food restaurants, ice-cold beer, women, and war stories. Besides visiting the famous naval battleship "Arizona" of Pearl Harbor fame, it was the sunny beaches, and all-night nightclubbing with two marine buds that filled three crammed, twenty-hour days; I don't actually remember sleeping. Having two R&Rs was indeed a privilege.

We thought we'd make up sleep losses on the plane. Flying back on Continental two hours out, on my side of the plane several of us noticed flames coming out of the engine and expressed concern to a flight attendant. Attentive but not visibly alarmed, she ambled up front in a stereotypical stewardess-esque strut. There was an announcement about a contained fire we should not worry about. A plane could operate without that one engine; in fact, it could operate satisfactorily on three, two if necessary, even only one in an absolute emergency. My window overlooked streams of bristling bright yellow.

Ten minutes later, a second message stated we'd be making an unscheduled stop in Guam, but we had to empty fuel tanks over water first. Dutifully pushing carts through, flight attendants finished handing out drinks and began lunch service with smiles and nonchalance as if this were routine while the plane maintained a circling maneuver to discharge fuel with wings dipping and stewardesses leaning rhythmically in harmony. The white fuel vapor cloud discharged from the wing on the opposite side and took more than an hour; the fire still did not go out. The pilot disclosed we were now operating on two engines as a precautionary measure.

Approaching Guam Airport, another one of the pilot's practiced baritone messages assured everyone not to be concerned about the fire (these things happen!) with details about how the fuel dump had been successful. Other indicators looked fine according to their follow-up announcement. Flight attendants buckled into their fold-down seats. The pilot's pleasant but authoritative voice added further instructions how it was important to be prepared beyond merely fastening seatbelts as an "abrupt" landing might produce "other situations" in such an emergency.

After cockpit commands about keeping heads down while hugging thighs, exiting the cabin safely, and finally how to protect your body in case of fire, our craft's tires touched the runway with squeaky bump-bumps, lurching markedly in a heavy left to right to left yaw before braking hard. The moment climaxed into slowing forward staggers. Inside the cabin, it was orderly and subdued.

I snuck a peek as we braked. Fire trucks lined the runway facing in every couple hundred feet or so, a dozen on both sides along with ambulances and other emergency vehicles, all with yellow lights flaring. As the jet decelerated, already-passed vehicles promptly moved into the jet's path to follow us, accelerating from a standstill to catch up to the Boeing 707. The plane halted with heavy metallic grunts and lunges in the middle of the runway. No buildings were in sight, just grass and lots of yellow flashes.

Everyone along the aisle stood up. Doors opened instantly positioning built-in stairs for descent as exiting processes began. We abandoned onboard paraphernalia as instructed. Row after row we filed toward a wall of humidity rushing in around us with disciplined composure. We all carried rounded eyes with poised delicate calmness. Efficiently funneling toward brightness, we ogled out little jet windows and saw clouds of white and black smoke emerging seconds before fire trucks closed in around us drenching the wing with billowing white sudsy stuff. By the time I descended exit steps, the process seemed nearly over, with large residual foamy puddle messes on the runway and no visible fire or smoke.

We were all escorted to buses and led away to a tiny terminal perhaps a half mile away.

Up Up and Away

We waited seven or eight hours before departing. No other planes used this terminal except for military fighters. Eventually we got back on the very same plane, retaking assigned seats. We were told the fire wasn't a serious matter and was easily fixed; the exterior had also been cleaned up and the plane moved nearer the terminal for routine boarding. With all else appearing otherwise normal, we took off amid numerous "what-if" conversations saturating every row. Gawking at the same wing, I speculated whether there might be a repeat performance.

Hypothesizing about airline fuel fires and precautions taken, we also talked about safety and the likelihood of this occurring again over water even though everything seemed like it was now performing normally. Although past midnight, dinner was served thirty minutes after takeoff. Engines railed, buzzed, and then purred. We were hungry and most of us sound asleep after desert. Our flight attendant with her usual broad smile took care of her duties as if nothing had occurred.

In a few hours, tires touching down at Da Nang awakened us; dawn seeping through fogged up windows already dripping from humidity. Without delay, we rendezvoused with transportation groups and ate breakfast. Heads groggy but with stories to tell, we were soon back in-country with early morning light escorting our reunions and jeep departures set for trekking into the heartland of our war-torn home away from home.

Steve's Letter

I had already known my buddy Steve wasn't stationed very far away from Hill 55. About five weeks ago I had been surprised to see his name on a WIA report in our office. Less than three weeks before going to Hawaii, I pulled some strings, volunteered for a "run" to Da Nang, and trekked to the Naval Hospital there to visit him. He'd been positioned just too close to some land mines and was recovering from shrapnel wounds. By now, he was in good spirits and ready to get back on the job. He said he'd see if he could make it out my way.

Later, just after I got back to Hill 55 from my Hawaiian sojourn, a hefty bag of full of our company's mail needed sorting …it was my job to sort these rubber-banded wads of envelopes into piles by platoon and distribute. On any particular day, one or two or maybe all three platoons could be in the field savoring rice paddy venues, scratching jungle rot inside their boots, or courting those pesky insects visiting them as they traipsed around on these nasty, often dangerous daily missions.

Today, there were three letters addressed to me, one from a girlfriend in Virginia, one from mom, and one from my old friend, Steve. I learned that after recovering, while on patrol Steve had volunteered to ride security on an Amtrac detachment from his in-field position to Hill 55 to visit me when he hit another ambush just a few thousand meters outside our perimeter …several men lost that day. For Steve, this time it again severely impacted his hearing. As a result of these two successive explosions, he suffered with Meneres disease and eventually lost the hearing of his left ear. Steve came home with two purple hearts. It would be years before our paths would cross again.

11

Remotest Outpost

April 1967

Having been assigned to Hill 55 for only seven months, by spring we could smell aromas changing in battalion's kitchen. We witnessed more choppers flying in and out and increased tensions. Bob Hope and Billy Graham had Christmas shows in Da Nang, but not right here like Jane Mansfield had. Fewer journalists were interviewing local brass. Temperatures were heating up as if something was in the oven, but the chefs weren't talking. Digesting news in the *Stars and Stripes* about DMZ campaigns, those skirmishes weren't on the menu here, but speculations about the DMZ were.

Daily, Lieutenant Centers made it a point to say Hill 55 was boring. Yet he began shifting his humdrum "Where's the action?" attitude when he read First Battalion Commander's intelligence reports. He didn't say what was stewing.

Next, I noticed fewer locals' tents among Vietnamese vendors outside the perimeter. Did they sense something too? We couldn't get haircuts anymore; some started chopping their "short cuts" inside our hooches. There were more frequent battalion checks on weapons, radios, even canteens and boots.

Yes, the kitchen was indeed heating up.

Boringness tiptoed into anxiety, greater edginess, and more officers' meetings. With a light in his eye, one afternoon Stormin' asked us to pack our duffels "real tight, just in case."

Offhand, "What if?" remarks impacted small talk with more, "Didjah hear 'bout's?" and, "Someone said's" than before. We anticipated news daily, but the only real new news occurred while eating at the mess hall, when we drank our warm beer, or took cold showers, or stayed awake on perimeter duty. Gunny told us to keep ready; officers said nothing—their jittery seriousness and wrinkly frowns probably concerned us more than protracted silence. But all those preoccupied mosquitoes did break the silence as they buzzed around their own dinners. We could at least accurately assess that particular distraction.

Stars and Stripes put good spin on the effectiveness of regional campaigns. Some battalions were being repositioned to Dong Ha; rumor was the Twenty-Sixth was going to be next for similar repositioning and indeed it was. Nobody knew where the village of Khe Sanh was going to be, except me of course. It was a small community as far north and as far west as one could get in South Vietnam, right smack on the Laotian border. The border with North Vietnam was the DMZ (demilitarized zone). When coupled with Laos, both were Viet Cong safe havens, which is why the Marine Corps and Army Special Forces had bases there.

Strategically, Khe Sanh lay on the main north-south trade corridor, route #9, that skirted the mountains and fed remote Montagnard villages on the eastern downslope. This tactically useful but still rather primitive regional passageway had been around for centuries, but now American troops at Khe Sanh blocked the previously discreet resupply habits. Word on the street was that the Gooks were seeking ways to reopen these supply routes for southbound contraband.

Northbounding Hazards

That's what I knew about Khe Sanh the morning that row of unanticipated helicopters had been readied for us to board on less than an hour's notice. These big whop-whopping machines were troop haulers, oversized fat choppers carrying crates and supplies as well as myriad undefined anticipations by all who were about to board them. Lt. Centers had just briefed us in a fast company meeting, giving us thirty minutes to get gear piled by these transport haulers on the runway. Pointed in his expressions, almost happy, he watched *his* troops assemble with unblinking eyes. We waited our turn to board the choppers, recognizing the frying pan, anticipating the fire.

Lifting off after no other fanfare, we flew over contorted squares of green, yellow, and brown paddies and skinny rows of tropical trees at good noisy whop-whop speed. About a dozen or more such choppers were transporting the Twenty-Sixth upcountry.

In my mind I noticed we flew diagonally to main roads and paddies, suggesting northwest bearing, something no one else was likely paying attention to. Greens were so very green, verdant, and so completely organized and repetitious on this visible ground quilt-like map, but with few people, animals or buildings. Round lakes and wide curling rivers displaced some of the paddies in the flatlands. Here and there were tiny villages of light-brown shacks, smoke wafting up, lining intersecting roads at junctions. Except for common corrugated, rust-colored metal roofs, there was an absence of anything else metallic. There were no water towers, storage bins, or warehouses. There were few structures, no paved roads, and very few vehicles.

Khe Sanh turned out not to be a particularly beautiful place. As we circled the landing site, surrounding areas were pockmarked with hundreds of reddish gray craters with water collecting from daily rain. Here the countryside looked used, abused, desolate, and war-landscaped. While there were dirt roadways, we saw no vehicles or bicycles, no signs of agriculture or commerce. Flanking the base were rolling hills void of much vegetation except for occasional scraggly trees and red clayish dirt, plus a pair of low mountains to the west.

In the din of helicopter blades and droning engines, no one talked. This northbound traverse created gripping moods as everyone absorbed information subconsciously. Furrowed foreheads and thin lips set a dark-urban tone of back alley trepidation. We unconsciously caressed our rifles, put our heads between our knees, or stared straight ahead and created resigned images. Heavy pensiveness prevailed amid drawn-down eyelids.

We had all heard stories about this place; *Stars and Stripes* printed scoops regularly. Officers told us how important it was going to be choking off that infamous route 9 corridor to win the war. We were now to be one of the solutions to that route 9 dilemma.

Touching Red Clay

We cautiously squinted our eyes. Once on the ground, we jumped underneath the chopper's not yet motionless blades, respectfully looking around to determine where to go, and what to do next.

We nervously scrutinized the comings and goings of those marines walking around. Most had reddish faces, sun-browned and sweaty, reflecting a metallic copper-colored complexion. I learned how this was a mark of tenure-type rank that paler guys honored.

Walking as directed in our neat and cleanly washed drabs to our new quarters, called hooches, we were not our usual cocky know-it-alls. Rows of once taut olive-green tents now sagged dirty sandy-red. Everything was slumped, low to the ground, dusty, and reinforced with empty ammo boxes and sandbags. Four-foot deep trenches flanked each tent. While the heat was less intense because of higher elevation, our moods were not.

Everything may have been orderly in Khe Sanh, but it was well worn, worn out, tired.

The attitudes generally displayed by those already wearing reddish-colored utilities were thoughtful and serious—more focused, more reserved than any of us newbies. Random social conversations were harder to detect between hooches or other buildings because so much "business" seemed to be going on.

As afternoon shadows lengthened, fewer marines even walked around. The mess hall was more subdued than what we were used to. In the evening, beer was rationed and warm. No one smoked cigarettes outside after the sun dropped behind gray curtains of mountains to the west. Or, if they did, they inhaled surreptitiously cupping the precious tobacco ember.

Everyone knew where to go without prompting. Outside, once dimness captured sky, there was a strange noiselessness between cannon firings; it was almost a respectful quiet one finds like at church. I'm not sure why everyone spoke so reservedly since nobody else could really overhear. Fifteen-second outgoing barrages were followed by minutes of whisperings.

Private Dialects

Every sentence had two prevailing words: "we" and "ready." Most communications, curiously, were abbreviated, composed of only three to five words, and were usually monosyllabic and resolute in tone. It was English but succinct.

"You guys get beer at mess?"

"Nah, you got cigs?"

"Nope, drag off this," handing him his hand-cradled half-used Marlboro. Preoccupied eyes glanced left and right repeatedly as if being watched while any further words were restrained. The Marlboro was privately sucked dry.

Miles inland, miles from Hill 55, and half a globe from home, I probably didn't appreciate the maturation process that was taking place for me at the time. Looking back now, maybe it was feeling like a sleepy caterpillar peeking out, anticipating first flight. Although it may have been just a next logical step, it now seems like it was an unraveling of cocoon-like encumbrances. There was a new abandonment of self for wherever olive-drab people and purposes were luring me.

Choice was not really part of this process except for the private reflections I shared with others exiting their own cocoons who shared this same special language. What I witnessed on the ground over the next four months added fluency to this new vocabulary and grammar.

While there was even more activity at Khe Sanh than anyone expected, there were also abundant stories written by sharp-eyed journalists and intellectual historians. Even dirty, gritty marines have written a few darned good stories too. For these military souls, such tales are uniquely theirs, of course, just like the fading tattoos or bleached, mottled skin they wear that others may or may not ever see.

12

Just Dust

Spring – Summer 1967

Wild, whining hums, clinks, clunks, cracks, and booms of some sort greeted the ear at Khe Sanh. Of course no one really listened to these dissonant symphonies of noxious noises from dawn to dawn. Acquiescing to eat, talk, and sleep through earsplitting gun firings, such sounds became monotonously unnoticeable, so no one talked about them either.

Perpetually, like strikes in a busy bowling alley, artillery guns randomly fired every two, five, or fifteen minutes, so the Viet Cong couldn't predict when firing would occur next or where rounds would likely fall. Every night such broken-record rackets and clamors were innocuously and continuously present amidst an almost inaudible, repetitive background cacophony of tin pans, distant rumblings of weapons fire, explosions, chopper whop-whops, or radio brouhahas. Dissonances cluttered up just inside the ear canal, but no one noticed or even remembered them five minutes later.

One time, however, the moon's solo dance captured an audience.

✪ ✪ ✪

Life in Prism

Lying face up on my cot, half dreaming, whims and impulses slid around in my head. I wrestled with my blanket. Being physically longer than the cot, repositioning shoulders, hips, or long feet, or in tonight's case my Achilles tendon to keep my position semi-comfortable above that wooden bar near the bottom, was an auto reflex. At least I slept on a stretched canvas cot; others often did not.

Though sweaty warm, scratchy blankets added comfort as I felt naked without *some*thing over me. Back in Illinois, my uncle had an army blanket we used camping. It was exactly like the olive green ones now on my bunk, but no *army* blankets here! No marine would ever call them *army* blankets! Most guys never used blankets, especially in May, except maybe as a pillow. This minute, my mood was calm, lulling, and thickly serene. I presumed a cool dream would have kicked back in by now, but my head churned like bread dough in a painless, slow-swirling, throb.

Linguistically, *cover* was marine lingo for hat, and I was daydreaming about a bunch of hats all over me in nonsensical ways. *Cover* was also an amusing word when uttered. Awake, I speculated about how balding marines used it to cover what they didn't want women to see. But to me, covers were really blankets.

Well, marines substituted words for lots of things such as referring sides of a tent as *bulkheads*. Floors were *decks*, which was obviously inaccurate on land anyhow. While these navy words may not have seemed right, we still verbalized them to be unique, not merely different.

But this is also why using *any*thing army-ish fell into this same thinking process; it made them not Marine Corps authentic, at least in the minds of authentic marines. Combining this with desires to participate in a good dream produced this senseless fantasy where *covers* turned into khaki hats inside nighttime dozing.

The odd throbs continued behind my eyes, an unclear reality against my will. Was it morning? Letting this warmhearted paralysis comfort me in the dark, there was a cool numbness around my forehead, like I had a helmet on while lying on the cot even though I didn't. My eyes were still dazed from incongruent fantasizing as I clutched hands behind my head. My eyelids remained semi-closed, contemplating layers of numbness between my fingers and my bread-doughy brain. I stretched, more awake than I wanted to be since it was still dark! Twitching eyelids kept opening on their own even though sleep-deprived.

I felt drugged.

Although there was no unnecessary illumination at night in Khe Sanh, it was never entirely dark either. Superfluous light inevitably crept inside tents, creating subtle, outrageous images that fed wild dreams and nightmares. Then there was the moon itself. My own quasi-paralytic silhouette was now becoming a rubbery shadow as I came to. I needed to take a piss; maybe in a minute I rationalized. Please, just one more minute. Freewill and inevitability competed.

Sleep was *so* very, very precious.

✪ ✪ ✪

Nighttime Daydreaming

Few of us hardly ever *saw* the enemy face-to-face. Besides these overzealous barrages of gun blasts every few minutes like a grandfather clock's pendulum banging sides of its interior panels, evidence of John-Wayne-type combat just wasn't there. Instead, there were frequent forays to two mountainsides (881N and 881S) overlooking route 9 or west to Lang Vei where the Special Forces camped. With one or two encounters a week, some were slight, some grim. There were efficient procedures for evacuees between corpsmen and aircraft. Just enough was going on to keep us serious-minded.

Sure, war was going on. Marines were hurt and killed. Medevacs dutifully transported the wounded. We witnessed insulated events that pressed us to keep serious demeanors as platoons patrolled. Transports roared in dropping tons of replenishments, food, water, ammunition, and, of course, replacement marines. Helicopters continuously whop-whopped in and out. There was gossip about friends of friends, about bad injuries, about blood. We did see and touch just enough of it, often enough, to be respectful. Our fears played out in nightmares. Seldom did we exchange emotional glances about these things.

We tended to look down at our boots instead when those offhand words circling in our heads weren't verbalized.

Notwithstanding a tedious in and out head-buzz, readiness prevailed. We knew our lines in this ever unfolding script with memorized responses that covered silent stress no one wanted to show. We knew buddies who went *out of country* from not too life-threatening wounds, and sometimes departure was in one of those slick, dark green-zippered bags. Such poignant reminders were everywhere, but we weren't obsessively preoccupied with them either. Omnipresent, they were the landscape on a big stage, part of that managed, judiciously distanced anxiety that everyone knew but hardly ever talked about.

For me, I understood the silent pains more when I noticed a trembling hand or overheard nightmare-induced dialogues or saw restrained tears when a marine just wanted someone to listen. More leather-skinned marines considered these reactions unmanly. For reasons I can't fully explain, many of those who were getting the just-get-over-it type comments needed an ear, and quite a few guys used mine to share their private thoughts.

Repetition, solitude, and boredom were everyday companions; we dealt with them in different ways without admission. First sergeant's, "just suck it up" remarks were anticipated when he was on stage. Consequently, sleeping was indeed a private haven, a retreat to savor every night, goddam banging clock pendulums or not!

But tonight was not to be an ordinary night.

Peekaboo Moon

Lights moved. One second it was pinpointed bright light, and the next gone, but reappearing in a slightly different spot. My half-open eyelids played tag with sporadic glimmers of brightness.

In this half-dreamlike state, I demurred it wasn't actually a flashlight but a gigantic, fat fluorescent mosquito. I didn't want to get up, but I perceived stiff odors and spicy smells like cumin mixed with dirt. I stretched my arms straight and frowned while I played with this slumbering numb wad of clump behind my eyes. I lengthened my legs downward, extending my arms as far as they could go, touching empty ammunition crates lining the tent. I massaged my Achilles on that wooden cot rod. I gained an inch of height doing this each morning. The numb, rubbery feeling started to abate . . . sort of.

At times like these when I couldn't think of anything else, instead of counting sheep I thought about maps to go back to sleep. The rural village of Khe Sanh was just a bit west, Laos several thousand paces west, and the DMZ a few miles north. It was effortless for me to envision how we all were tucked snugly in the upper left-hand corner of this skinny, serpentine-shaped, tropical country. As strategic as maps geographically suggested, and as much as *Stars and Stripes* reported, nothing especially weighty had happened of late, at least not since the Twenty-Sixth had arrived. According to Lt. Centers, it was Hill 55 all over again.

Arms clutching neck, my eyes decided it truly *was* the moon, and it *was* moving like moons do. Detecting where the moon must next be as it moved over the tent, I saw brightness shine in like flashes of light casting eerie shadows. It was curiously bright especially in predawn, as one is slowly extracted from deep, much needed rest into this numb-bubbling moonshine thing I was swimming in. Embracing my blanket, I consented to waking up with another pointed toe-stretch. For inexplicable reasons, my head just wouldn't move; this heavy painless "bulge" lay right between my nested palms and a swooshing brain.

Oh please, give me another few minutes of slumber.

But what was that smell? My moist nose stuck together on this edge of lingering pungent aromas amid odd, heavy, peaceful cerebral fog. Coming to, I glanced at neighboring cots by rolling my literally unliftable head to one side. Pete's cot was no more than eighteen inches away, and I noticed no one was there sleeping. He must've been taking a leak or something.

Rude Awakening

I sifted a dozen things in my rubberized head, which began infusing hot blood. There was heat behind my ears as my face chilled dry. There was *not one other person* in any of the other six cots, none at all, just me, alone!

A full moon lulled pensively inside the tent. No, I was eyeballing Mr. Moon through a big hole! I could see little points of lights too! Stars? Was I outside or inside?

Rolling sideways, I jerked my head off the cot by elevating my shoulders, then grabbed my glasses twisting them onto my nose, and went into a half-seated, one-elbow-on-the-cot position. I didn't realize my mouth was open until I felt saliva dripping out. In five heart pounds, a mindboggling, thick, utterly muffled stillness swathed my face. I looked peripherally in one hundred eighty degree jerks from left to right.

I took a deep, gurgling, gulping breath and inhaled saliva. I tried to listen and smelled fresh herbal aromas again right smack in front of me like fresh gunpowder. It all must have been just there, just then! My heart involuntarily hammered veins full of panic-pumping blood in another hot flash of chilling hysteria. Biceps in my temples pushed up my head where it hadn't intended. My gut muscles shivered in disbelief.

Already fully dressed (we always slept with our clothes on except for boots), I cocked my head upward, slightly afraid to move yet afraid to stay put. I zeroed in on how the full moon created bizarre shadows inside the tent. My mind raced . . . no, it lumbered erratically like rocks sliding down a hill . . . seeking shaded but familiar in-the-dark enemies.

Two or three further blood thumps passed before I was able to sit all the way up, listening for cues as toes slammed the deck. Was that a bird I heard? A bird at night? And then I jostled one femur up braced by a shaky knee, brain hazy, steadying myself to a tent pole as each of my senses overlapped. I thought I heard distant voices but fell back onto the cot then stood again. My brain finally jerked alert.

I remained standing, two size 14s planted on a dirt deck semi-ready to ante up on this table of unknowns.

Where *was* everybody?

"Hullo?" I questioned naïvely.

Nervously swaying, I straightened my body, hugged tent poles for balance, and stared at . . . full shadows *inside* the tent! My dilated eyes discovered more and more detail even through dirty glasses. With brain declotting, vision joined sudden alertness. Leaning toward the tent flap while holding two tent poles, I threw the flap open and observed something I had never ever witnessed before.

It was strikingly eerie, like a sci-fi or vampire or Frankenstein movie. It was serenely gelled quiet, moon bright. There were no guns, no repetitious firings, no noise whatsoever . . . only this hum-hissing sound in my head.

My eyes stared.

White Ocean

As far as I could see in all directions was a thick cloudy layer of pure white dust about waist high that enabled rather creepy and uncanny undulations to list and flow, otherwise bearing little motion. It looked like a huge sea of vacillating, misty, supernatural water with glowing white trees sticking out. Above the fluorescent dust layer was clear black sky, full moon and profuse radiating stars as blunt witness. That spicy smell of cumin-laced gunpowder saturated my dream-laden senses that were still coming to.

I embraced the tent pole to keep myself from falling. My concentration wobbled along with my under-responsive arms and legs. I felt like I was breathing underwater. An ocean of dust reflected a judicial moon umpiring tranquility...legitimizing but overwhelming. No, it was not serene at all. It had become eerily alien as consciousness swam in slow motion above a surreal sea of powdered white dust. It was calm terror.

Coming-to was not an instant process. I was no longer dreaming but standing, bewildered, alone, and conspicuous.

In the next two or three seconds, I heard gagging, guttural yells in the distance, "Carmen! Carmen, o'year!" These trailing sounds were oddly inaudible as if they were wrapped in flannel. I heard sounds again, two simultaneous, higher pitched, still shrouded, distant, overlapping voices hollering echoed words like, "Ampin! Ampin!" and "Helmy! Helmy!" and "Inking!" I felt as if I were in a tunnel.

The white ocean began undulating slowly with its upper surface disappearing into fly-away wisps. As disassembled pieces of my mind reconnected, I translated, "Carmen" into "Corpsman! Corpsman! Over here!" I tried standing without holding onto the tent pole, my legs further apart to assure stability.

Air started moving. Hearing faint rumbling in the distance, like one of those approaching Illinois thunderstorms with low-pitched whistling like what jets sound like at airports, it broke to silence again. There were no real airplane sounds, no guns, just repeating underground rumbles, far-off yellow flashes of bright light, vibrations, and hissing as my mind translated, "Ampin" into captain, "helmy" into help me, and "inking" to incoming!

Swimming in mental slow motion stew, nauseating slips of stuff churned in my belly. I finally yelled out a gurgled, "H'lo! Anybody here?" Not knowing what else to cry out or do in these three or four more heartbeats, I stepped outside with a shaky gait but could see not one other person as layered dust nimbly heaved way into nothingness, dispersing with my movements through ever-so-slight tresses of moving air.

"Hey jerk-head, g'down here," came a high-pitched screaming retort fifteen feet away, "We got fuckin' incoming."

This was the real thing! I hunched over and ogled the shadowy long black rectangle where our foxhole lay. Despite a semi-clotted mindset, I dove with a slow motion gymnastics maneuver into the trench positioned aside our tent semi-gracefully rolling with a fleshy warm thud onto the very top of a heap of live breathing bodies.

A typical trench between four and five feet deep and a couple feet wide at most, it completely compacted a dozen to fifteen huddled marines garbed out with flak jackets, hand grenades, rifles, and sweat. At the far end, a few helmets on top looked like a bed of seashells. No one talked, though there were stifled grunts and groans from marines at the bottom I presumed upon my grand flat entrance...it was a bonding experience.

Coincidently, I then heard a rush and swoosh of more incoming that sounded like landing transport jets, then crashes of distant but not-too-distant explosions, one after the other steadily growing louder yet still flannelled inside my nonexistent rubber helmet. The North Vietnamese's mortars were being walked in toward us, but reverberations were still distant enough, maybe a hundred or more yards away, slowly growing louder, intimidatingly closer every two or three seconds.

I had nothing on my feet but socks, no weapon, no helmet, and no flak jacket. There was just the back of my olive-drab T-shirt facing that neon moon, now frowning near the Laotian horizon, and me barely below ground level.

Eventually these distant explosions grew dimmer as the heavy pendulum of our guns resumed; it was a solemn drum banging mixed with what was probably the sound of incoming mortars at that point pounding the other side of the clock. Then it all stopped, again creating that numbing, eerie, silence in my ear canals.

There were screams, and then high-pitched screeches imploring, "Help!" Shouts of, "Captain!" Moans of, "Over here!" Why hadn't I heard them as clearly before? They were human, but they were still muffled.

After I had opened my eyes from deep sleep to now punching my nose down onto two hand grenades on the butt of a marine's webbed belt probably took less than a minute at most. Nonetheless, this human-soft trench was my new home. This recently found, smelly pile of humanity was bizarrely comforting, solidly warm with mutually felt security albeit numbly sensed, pasted together for the identical needed purpose of common survival.

Those rapid incoming explosions had approached then stopped, blanketed voices became more frequent and audible, more active, more understandable. Once incoming silence returned and lingered, there were detectible vibrations underground and deliberate but cautious movement out of the trench, one layer at a time me being first. A methodical, nonstop flow of marines crawled upward, out, and stood up in a low stoop with hunched-down shoulders. Eyes seized information as dawn-cooled breezes evaporated sweat.

With no helmet, weapon, or flak jacket, I shivered, exposed and defenseless amid this crowd. I huddled, confused about what next to do.

Repositioning

Marines now scurried nearby, darting toward the cries for help. In the next thirty seconds, we saw lights flashing amidst intense human expressions bearing groans of acute pain. Corpsmen rapidly maneuvered their wares like basketball players, bustling around flailing officers to access human objectives. Officers inaudibly refereed traffic with hand gestures and subdued commands. Other marines assisted in moving the injured with uncanny speed and care.

By then, the white ocean was completely gone and a different serenity was taking its place. The process for our little huddled group to disperse to preset stations began seconds later, except for Pete and me.

Dusty haze lightened the east. Although we realized it might begin again, we unanimously and privately knew we had to get out of the trench to do *some*thing. There wasn't anyone to give permissions or orders as the last ones out from the trench finally emerged amid remaining grunts, profanities, and unanswerable questions toward each other.

"Wuhappened?" I asked as we reentered the tattered tent for my M-16, flak jacket, and helmet. I straightened my gait.

"Damned if I know. Jeez. It hit so goddam fast." Both Pete and I booted up and finally hustled off to preassigned bunkers near the perimeter where we gained more news.

"My ears are ringing."

"You okay?" he asked.

"Huh? I guess so. My head seems a little out of whack."

Trying to hurry helped circulate the blood in my legs, and I bounced along right behind Pete without struggling, recognizing how wobbly my gait still was. The fact that I had actually slept through the barrage was only now sinking in. Just how could that have occurred? Pete and I shared shudders with others about what-if questions.

"Didja see second platoon?" Pete asked anyone who'd listen. "Didja see that crater? Did anyone make it?"

That dust layer had been stirred up and dissipated quickly. Mr. Moon was now kissing the horizon; hints of dawn grew noticeably brighter by the time we got to our post. It was a new day. Repeating big guns resumed, officers' commands became more animated, frequent, and forceful. The white ocean was a result from that first wave of mortars exploding near us, settling during the immediate silence following then coalescing in that layer until we all disturbed it upon exiting the trench. That dust ocean probably lived for mere minutes and few others ever even saw it. The ordnance odor lingered omnipresent amidst voices rushing around to help those in need.

We commiserated about those who we knew were hit and learned later many died. I became pensive about the event. It wasn't exactly loss of life that made it a moment of deliberation; death had occurred before. Instead, it became personalized about how it involved me individually and the intimacy of my rather statuesque role . . . my invisible helmet . . . the dust. I leaned back against sandbags, withdrawing from vulnerabilities surrounding me in the bunker, and let my mind seek its own course naturally, submitting to comfort of mental distance from realities at hand as Pete continued to commiserate with the other two in low not-to-be-overheard tones. I was transfixing into a survival mode uniquely mine to use.

My head numbness thinned. My gait was okay, and I bore no visible wounds.

When the sun came up, most marines acted on anxieties and lack of sleep. Though little typical military chatter, there was a whole lot of say-nothing small-talk that was probably only used to elicit a response. I did it too. It was a way to confirm you and the person you were talking to were both still alive without actually using those kinds of words.

I eyeballed everything outside the perimeters, nothing could be seen at tree line but we stared resolutely. "Charlie" wasn't expected; but we still shared the duty. Tension overrode fatigue.

This bunker location was safe and appropriate to marshal thinking right then, to rearrange what emerged in disarray, letting the moment's anesthesia do its bidding within a needed massaging of soul. No one interrupted these acts of regaining composure; few sounds really interrupted at all. Despite pendulum banging every few minutes, it remained otherwise quiet inside the bunker and inside my mind. Writhing thoughts gradually recovered to consider things more practical than reactive.

My breathing was deep, my aloneness right now a comfortable blanket to savor.

Aftermathmatics

I found out later that there were two separate incoming barrages. Twenty-Sixth's second platoon was hit directly inside their "safe trench" on first poundings. That was the one I had slept through...the very one that occurred about two or three car lengths away from my bedazzling dreams and army-blanket comfort just prior to witnessing the full moon's traverse...the one that propelled whizzing shrapnel above, beside, and through every standing object in the tent...the one that seared second platoon flesh and bones with cumin spice and deadly bloody condiments tossed randomly about. And I was perfectly clean, unscented, unscathed, and deaf to it all.

In second platoon's trench, those nearest points of mortar impact were dead. There were four. Those next nearest received severe shrapnel wounds inflicting internal injuries; these half dozen marines were swiftly transported to choppers. Even so, half died in a day or two as well. The next group had various injuries. Most of these were evacuated promptly, all in a day or two; they all recovered and then went home. A handful returned to support forming a new Second Platoon. *Everyone* in Second Platoon got something lasting that night *plus* a Purple Heart later but, I heard *none* of these intimate intrusions though impact points were mere steps away from my wafting sleeping body.

Shrapnel from that initial barrage leveled second platoon's tent, created several craters, went on to extensively penetrate our two tents. Debris was strewn everywhere. I pondered Mr. Moon's role in all this alongside hot killing shrapnel surely whizzing inches from my face to create all those moon holes...tattered open slits, and black edged slashes in the sides of gnashed-out tents. The same shrapnel surely must've electrified my dream state as I coddled my blanket and embraced a silent protective semi-schizophrenic journey.

Everyone scurried to designated dugouts of safety, just as we all were supposed to do. They surely must have been wildly yelling aloud, "Incoming, incoming." I struggled with thoughts about being left alone sleeping, and then waking and smelling spicy dirt odor with no one noticing my occupied bunk.

I inched out of this conflicting guilt of having survived versus being abandoned. I wondered what mattered. One half of me spoke, the other half of me listened. At times like these, and not just for me, private time was, well, broodingly private as I contemplated irreconcilable values of luck and fate.

Then I pondered more about those openings between me and the moon, including those shrapnel holes on the side of the tent at eye level and nearby mortar craters! I felt like I was in court. How could I *not* sense what was happening? In that first barrage, I had done *nothing* to help myself as I naïvely slept through testimonies of all the others, and no one else thought to wake me as they panicked; yet I was serendipitously spared! Was a jury pronouncing "not guilty" in this chamber?

I explored heavier competing concepts like guilt v. responsibility or duty v. debt among many yet-undefined roles to come. *Just dust* matters less than a just dust does.

I wouldn't leave the courtroom until months later, as normalcy eventually wove itself back into typical distractions. Despite carrying this kind of introspective soul baggage, I emotionally could not unload it or explain it very well.

13

Male Mail Mileage

June – August 1967

This was A Company, First Battalion, Twenty-Sixth marine regiment. There were three "grunt" platoons and a weapons platoon with second lieutenants in charge of each. I was a member of headquarters platoon, comprised of a commanding officer (CO), executive officer (XO), gunnery sergeant (Gunny), first sergeant (Top), admin chief, and two lance corporal gophers (me being one, the other being my cohort Bierne who would have rather posed for Marine Corps recruiting posters than keep track of carbon paper and rubber bands). Five platoons altogether usually meant about seventy-five to a hundred men, depending on turnover.

My skill was the typewriter, and I was pretty darned fast and accurate, so paperwork naturally fell to me. No C-plus-iosis infected *these* ten fingers!

Starting on Hill 55, house duties were augmented to sort and deliver mail. With Bierne on more patrols with Lt. Centers here in Khe Sanh, my headquarters type duties expanded further. Centers didn't like me much, so I didn't get paddy water or mud in my boots that much once he took over as CO except maybe when it rained.

Our experiences in Khe Sanh matured. Events occurred nearly every other day. There were more choppers whop-whopping in and out, more patrols up Hill 881N and 881S, more platoons on missions into nearby jungle valleys, more crater evidence, more vehicle dents, more casualties and KIAs, even more noises, explosions, yes, even a few invisible rubber-head wraps of mine returning now and then with more sleepless nights and weird dreams.

Incoming Mail

For me, one job led to another. With casualties increasing, there was more to do with those wounded or who were killed in action, like writing letters of condolence, inventorying personal belongings not unlike on the USS Vancouver the summer before but more complicated and more regularly. Onboard ship or on Hill 55, not much time was sacrificed for these tasks because KIAs and WIAs were relatively few. Now personal belongings were multilayered with months of accumulation, more confounding, more subtle. Gunny and I kept putting ourselves in the shoes of mom and dad who would be receiving these packages. What might matter most to them was thoughtfully deliberated.

Postmarks of the last arriving correspondence documented exactly when news was disclosed to parents or spouse...for us, a second demise. Thinking about presence and absence of soul, or what love meant within handwritten lines of script or photographs along with my own anticipatory eyes looking through someone else's camera, I became careful about my own penned words when writing home. I stopped asking for pictures; I stopped taking pictures.

One time while reading these letters I observed that an injured marine who lost his legs (he later died of wounds) had more than one wife and both were writing to him, creating issues about to whom to send the CO's condolence letter (or letters), and to whom to return his personal effects. We speculated about who would ultimately collect the military life insurance. Having to make a decision, Lt. Centers wrote his letter to the mother. We learned weeks later they did find out who the first wife was; it was she who received the insurance check.

No longer a new "boot" (our word for rookie), my size 14s were caked with red clay on worn soles...my discolored drabs dusty reddish olive, and my utility cover sweat-stained with white blotches of crusty dried salt showing up around band and brim.

Assignments . . . and moods . . . evolved yet further.

Vital Eye

As replacements for KIAs and wounded joined A Company in increasing numbers, most didn't get to know each other very well very quickly, so there were daily introductions and frequent reintroductions; I was part of this process. After handshakes I'd ask newbies, "What state are you from?" and I'd have something to say about wherever it was. No NCO or officer could engage in this type of welcoming question like I could.

It wasn't much of a further stretch to grasp how Gunny, Top, or officers couldn't often recognize newly injured or those recently killed, especially when unconscious troops came in groups of five or six or were separated from others who knew them. These groups inevitably would include the rawest recruits. Some receiving-tents became temporary warehouses of bodies, staged for prompt removal by transport planes having no other purpose. There was an odd but unforgettable odor associated with the dead; a sweet, decaying aroma twisted our stomach muscles. Everyone recognized it.

Since I delivered mail daily, it ended up improbably that occasionally I was the *only* one at hand who could recognize what everyone else looked like! As bodies of KIAs or radically injured were processed, it sometimes became expedient for my signature to go onto papers identifying who had died or who was being dutifully escorted away or transported unconscious to a cargo plane for transport back to a hospital.

When identification chains, or dog tags, were missing either from a sense of bad luck some guys held for them or for the clinking noise they could produce when worn free around the neck or from the severity of profoundly heavy trauma to the head or neck, it became a matter of accurate and immediate processing; I saved other people time and frustration with my knack for positive recognition.

Psychologically, many were having trouble with the sheer volume of those dead or dying or in the presence of blood and missing body parts, but I was able to rekindle that now useful distancing mechanism, so I was pegged as the right person for several jobs no one else wanted anything to do with. For me, instead of thoughts of anger or revenge or despair, there was a useful rationalization process that connected natural cause and effect but without any emotional connection. Instead of sadness, I called upon respectful acquiescence at arm's length under circumstances such as these. It was personal yet it was not. For KIAs, I coordinated these duties with a battalion unit called "graves registration," which didn't allow much time to squander.

Since patrols near route 9 or on both Hill 881 north and south took hits once or twice a week, busy Lt. Centers always took time to chat with me about marines who were "leaving" or "gone." Understanding the value of his work specialty, he was a demanding but passionate man about his military mission and achievements; he knew he was unique among peer officers, both in appearance *and* delivery. When typing letters of condolence for him to sign, including letters for two lieutenants who were killed inside of six weeks, I remember he'd ponder his ball point for a moment of reflection, pressing lips and closing his eyes before slowly lowering the pen to sign each communication in a deliberate, hard-pressed, neatly penned "Norman B. Centers" signature.

Witnessing others' reactions, I detected the typical military protocols expressed by Gunny, Top, and other battalion "tenureds" were wearing thin. I assumed they tried to isolate themselves from personalizing too many of their troops injured or dead, so many of whom they didn't even know or recognize, their human feelings privately disguised to everyone else . . . this was how one's skin got "leathered."

Then there were tactical challenges related to high troop turnover, like impromptu assessments of marines' abilities or attitudes, ostensibly to elevate chances for success on specific missions, or to bring into line certain personalities with certain needed skills. Back in the corner, I was privy to many of these hush-hush conversations from strengths and weaknesses and ultimately to collective vulnerabilities.

Though it was totally military-oriented, there would be snide remarks about majors or colonels up the chain of command who apparently (according to some officers at least) didn't know much about what they were asking for; yet missions from these decision makers were honored without hesitation. Perhaps they were just venting? I don't know very much about military strategy, but it seemed consequential choices were often made for strange or unsupportable reasons just because so-and-so wanted it or because something was cancelled and this would do.

People paused but ignored blood on the ground or on clothes. Yet I could perceive these pauses and how eyes would squint and lips purse. Then there was loss of camaraderie like we had onboard ship and during the early months in-country; it became all business. Few people took time to know anyone else's first name except for me, of course, because I did the mail.

Food was sustenance. It wasn't delicious if it had any taste at all, just fuel. Showers were necessary and welcomed distractions when we could get them. We somehow knew when it was our turn. Those shiny, empty, dark green bags that would inevitably become the means to go home for so many of our colleagues, were stacked in neat piles of plastic at the back of certain tents, necessary inventory. We kept counts on these.

Wide-eyed helicopter pilots hovered for just a minute while their shaking craft was loaded once again with those who lost the bet. The pilots rudely yelled for marines on the ground to do their job faster with a "we-don't-have-all-day" attitude that appeared inappropriate to some of us who saw it as more self-serving than a concern about cargo. Never shutting off their engines, they wasted no time flying back through clouds of chopper powder to safer havens. Then again, I did understand their anxieties too and the uncertainties of the situation. Each of us had different missions whether or not they understood ours. Yet we did have our own "they-sure-have-it-easy" retorts feeling a little underappreciated.

While mission remained acute, human purpose eroded.

Gritty red dust clouds swirled.

Envious Departures

Sticky-hot days of June and July slopped into the sultry days of August. Incoming mortar-type events had become more regular during July and August but nothing came close (to me at least) as that overwhelming mortar event now two months past that devastated so much here at Khe Sanh. My disconcerting dizziness returned from time to time, but that odd thick-helmet numbness had mostly worn off after a couple of weeks and only recurred for very short periods of time after that. I learned to live with it when it visited.

Typical cargo aircraft(C-130) at Khe Sanh.

On the last week of July, that unique but too close-in swooshing noise happened yet again. On the day before Sergeant Sanders was due to leave Khe Sanh, he was killed as he slept with others wounded nearby. As I examined the riddled tent, a crater lay open beside a shredded cot and packed bag readied for the journeys home.

Sanders' shiny green body bag was prepared for transport the next morning on the very same plane he'd have used to depart as a passenger. Emotional poignancies of Sanders' tent lingered in synapses above and behind my forehead as my own departure date was nearing, a couple weeks away.

For us marines traversing the Pacific westbound in July 1966 who remained active, alive, and unwounded, August 1967 signified our month of departure. So, as my own twelfth month turned into my thirteenth in-country, and weeks-left envies evolved into days-left jealousies, I officially became a short-timer myself, "one of *those*."

Two days before "the date," I processed into A Company ten newbies right off the plane in crisp olive drabs who had already heard about our recent incoming events. Their eyes were wide and round, absorbing every single word on my checklist...every word of advice, every casual remark I made. The day was intense. Red dust started to cake on foreheads with humidity's glue as their own baptism ceremony took hold blessing most of them for their own thirteen to come.

My reddish-olive-green canvas duffel bag was packed solid-tight the night before, just as Cpl. Sanders' had been. My bunkmate Pete said, "you're lucky, man. I got two more months in this goddam forsaken place."

"I'm not countin' chickens yet." We both were thinking about Sanders.

"Yeah . . . I'm just not sure if I'm gonna make it outta here . . . in one piece. The odds are . . ." Pete shook my hand as his words trailed off.

I read his eyes.

Exodus

On the morning of, I turned in my rifle, ammo, flak jacket, and helmet. I survived a short checklist of things to do, said a few good-byes with a few "take-me-with-you" handshakes, and boarded a silver transport plane headed for Da Nang Airport.

My job was done. But right now, all I could think about were eyes . . . the eyes from those who wanted to be me that day. And, it was my turn to leave them behind.

Rice paddies were visible out the window. My inner self began what I might call a cleansing process...a process of dismissal or liberation or perhaps emancipation as I narrowed my attention onto what was yet to come despite lingering red dust on my pants and red grit under my fingernails. I again breathed deeply, bathing in this process without any smiles...just with my intellectual flannel blanket for comfort.

Although another page would turn for Khe Sanh, another different page would turn for me.

14

Pacification Process

August 1967

A completely full plane flew us the same day to Okinawa where we were able to shower, clean up, and put on a new khaki summer dress uniform. Everyone wanted to look sharp. We waited a few tedious hours before boarding a Continental jet bound for southern California with a refueling stop at Travis AFB near San Francisco. The all-night flight was mesmerizing for me as I recalled memories of Guam thirty-five thousand feet below (no fire detected on this plane's wing!). We all felt safe and excited with expectations for welcome-home events. Some slept, others were wide-eyed and eager to experience anticipated freedoms to come.

I knew there'd be welcome-homes for me too. I told Mom and Dad I'd call from L.A. and let them know when to expect me. With fingernails now clean and clipped along with my Okinawa haircut, I felt complete in spirit. I stretched my legs, listening affectionately to engine noises muffled by a couple hundred marines gaining back some of that precious sleep, but my own eyes joined the wide-eyed group.

Relaxing in a mentally spatial map-oriented abandon, like only I can do, my vision recollected on how thirteen months ago I looked westbound to the Philippines via Hawaii on the bridge, then southbound to "Normandy," then northbound up the coast of Vietnam, then southwest to Hill 55, northwest to Khe Sanh, and now eastbound across the Pacific. It was fascinating in other ways as well. I watched ships' lights below. My map head clicked back in with lines of longitude passing quickly beneath me, doubling the day but "losing" hours, one at a time. August 12 was over forty hours long that year!

Three of us who were awake were permitted to enter the cockpit and speak with the captain. He described instruments in detail explaining how he knew where planes were by looking at a green fluorescent screen on his dashboard. Actually, the pilot was probably bored. When a peek of lighter sky rapidly emerged in the east, we returned to our seats.

I didn't sleep at all. Then we landed. My eyes just stared out the window at airport paraphernalia, early morning baggage transporters, other planes, scurrying workers, shiny glass windows on terminal buildings, other real buildings in the distance, and even some real homes. My mind was shifting gears as images clicked into place. Uncannily, events in Vietnam having occurred not forty-eight hours ago seemed to have happened months ago…if they actually happened at all. It felt like a book had been placed back on its shelf. Examining cracks in the concrete out my window, I thought about those sidewalk cracks in that San Diego neighborhood.

As the plane took off a second time bound for El Toro (USMC) Air Base near Los Angeles, the sensation wasn't the same. I leaned back and thought about dust and nodded into dozes until the landing gear touched down. Disembarking, I paused and looked around, trying not to lose the serenity of the moment under the kind and comforting arm of sunshine wrapped around my shoulder. I scrutinized painted white lines and black cracks on asphalt, making sure I didn't break my mother's back on weathered tarmac below my just-polished shoes.

We were hustled off and separated into groups depending upon what airline we were assigned and our next destination. I was paired with a marine flying to Oklahoma City, and TWA stopped in Albuquerque en route. We both called our families then boarded. I slept for ninety minutes on that less than one hour flight home . . . and it was *still* August 12.

It was as if there was no war going on at all. Vietnam didn't exist; McDonald's did.

Retrospection and Re-assimilation

My timing entering and departing Vietnam was what it was. No, I may not have been the rebel I thought I was when Steve and I made our mutual pledge twenty two months prior, but I was no longer that wimp I once thought I was either. Who could have predicted I would have gained so much life perspective by this journey? Unlike countless others in Khe Sanh who would go on to hand over their bodies less than six months later, I survived serendipitously to traverse quite a few more stories yet to come.

I repetitiously reviewed the new pages in my mental scrap book.

I never did drive tank. Neither my muscles nor my sweat ever did look like those resolute guys on the recruiting posters. But, Steve sure called the shot correctly when he said we didn't go half-way either.

I had viewed bodies of KIAs regularly, but I also remember being thereafter relieved for all slightly-wounded marines …those who could fly home inside a plane instead of in a cargo hold. Their in-country stint was thus shortened and often their take-home pride and self-value of contribution expanded. On the other hand, others more severely injured became disfigured, disabled . . . even deactivated from anticipated life yet to come. While appreciation of nearby witnesses and rallying Americans vigorously supported so many patriotic philanthropists, the lives of these WIAs would be forever changed in unimaginable ways.

But, yet others among those ostensibly able-bodied who remained were the *uncounted* injured who bore no physical wounds, no obvious suffering, no detectable distress at all. They shouldered their smiles amid stories never shared; they disconnected their eyes from invited conversations; they acquiesced to internal concessions they carried only within themselves . . . concessions they could not admit to anyone, friend or not.

For months, my unconsciousness had witnessed these wisps and threads of trauma nightly until my own emotions dulled beneath a self-defensive body armor invisible to everyone else. Was it merely fatigue? Or, submission? Surrender? Theft?

Maybe all wars are like that, I'm just not sure; but, my own education had already been stained with the trivialized blood of others and their many pensive untold stories. I learned. My body armor thickened. I adapted. Emotions became untrustworthy. I survived.

I played the script assigned me with pride, insight and choice. There are so many who have experienced greater intensity and consequences while there are yet others who didn't survive at all. Sometimes the gifts we receive are not appreciated until much later.

Was it justice? Or was it mercy?

Had my eyes changed too?

15

Bars and Stripes

October 1967

Finally arriving in Washington, D.C. after a month's leave in Albuquerque plus travel time to the East Coast, I checked in as my orders directed, carrying a duffel packed with more brand new civvies than marine khakis, thanks to Mom and Dad. My old stuff just didn't fit; besides, bell-bottom trousers were now in style. I can't remember being so well fed with Mom's best for so many consecutive days in a row.

Most of my uniforms had been heavily soiled, badly tattered, lost, or stolen. I needed more of just about everything. I had packed the two summer-dress uniforms that could be switched back and forth. Fortuitously, winter-dress was coming due in a week so I still had time to get all my replacements.

Having little else except olive-drab T-shirts and underwear, socks, and one pair of scuffed shoes, I also had one good tie for my summer-dress khakis, a web belt and my piss cutter. I had thrown away all my war-worn drab utilities; these couldn't be worn stateside anyhow. Hauling a few pieces of *tenured* wardrobe around plus my civvies, this portable canvas bag would do for suitcase storage a few more days. This war-riddled duffel carried everything in the world I owned.

Except, that is, for my brand new 1967 black Volkswagen, promptly no longer new from this two thousand mile cross-country trek, but shiny, clean and economical nonetheless. It reflected a new start on several levels. With a duffel fitting easily under the hood with plenty of room for stacks of AAA maps, my head had already been readied for four days' worth of therapeutic map gorging.

But this day I was walking into my new duty station, military street-savvy and content to be back among traffic jams and neon lights. After over a year of too little independence, my whizzing a couple thousand miles across the homeland made me feel two inches taller and proud. Ah, how freedom swells the heart and elevates one's spirit!

Paraphernalia and Rigmarole

Piss cutter. I believed I knew why it bore this name because there was a front to back "V" channel along the top crease. Theoretically that little pleat was tight enough to *cut* or to route a stream of piss. Calling them piss cutters or covers (we *never* said *hat*) was sufficient to completely forget what its proper name was. The real *why* I didn't know, but it was always worth an internal chuckle.

What I did know was that after Vietnam, I was both prepared and looking forward to doors opening up. Despite stories documenting hassles and fusses guys went through getting processed into the D.C. bureaucracy, that stuff seemed foreign to me since I had been planning ahead. I intended to start orientation processes the next day once I reported in, ate dinner, and got a place to sleep. I could get uniforms, housing, etc. before reporting to my new unit. After getting my haircut, piss cutter neatly in place, shoes cleaned up, I presented myself exactly on time at Henderson Hall, standing tall, weathered, copper-skinned, and proud, orders in hand.

"Are you Corporal Choc?" asked a top sergeant while reading my orders with what seemed unusual concentration as he frowned openly over wire-rimmed glasses. Beside my orders was a thin red file folder with my name on it.

After my year across the water, this NCO looked more like a stereotypical government civil servant than a marine. The title "top" was a friendly rank name used colloquially for first sergeants by other marines to distinguish rank for more than just a sergeant and to avoid having to say "first sergeant," a more formal term, when speaking to or about him. Glancing toward me, he arched his heavy hairy eyebrows, contorting them into a condescending half-cocked stare.

"Yes, sir," I said attentively. I didn't need to say "sir" of course, but top's carefully ironed shirt looked officer-ish, and right away I could tell he liked the word "sir." I best not say *top* yet; after all, this *was* Washington, D.C.! But he continued to mull, flipping pages, and glancing toward me repeatedly, up and back, back and forth, as if waiting for me to say something more. His pen rubbed a snickering upper lip.

"I have a note here, odd, hmmm, doesn't make sense," he said opening the red file, "It's initialed by, oh yeah, 'Staff Sergeant Williams.' Well, I do know *him*." But Top didn't ask any questions as he leafed through the documents, licking his fingers again and again to turn pages.

Standing at ease, I waited and waited.

Relaxing back, digesting paperwork, he looked up at me and then looked down at papers again, eyeing me over the rim of his glasses. He was thinking about what to say.

I adjusted my piss cutter under my belt. At least he could ask me to sit; he didn't. I examined the office's furnishings: US Marine Corps and American flags, photographs, framed certificates, and a small brass sculpture of the Iwo Jima Monument with a tiny red, white, and blue flag. But as neat as walls, tables, and other furnishings were, the desk itself was cluttered, stacked with manila file folders and newspapers, strewn pens paperclips, plus a stapler and a scotch-tape dispenser used as paperweights.

While "at ease" is a military position that means resting while standing, my body was now rigid, and only my eyes moved around the room. My head persisted in an "at-attention" mode, not knowing what else to do. So this must have been one of those hassles I had been told about.

My uniform was clean but disheveled-looking since I had already worn it a few times, thus it bore many telltale folds and creases. My second uniform was packed and undoubtedly just as rumpled; I had no time to get anything cleaned or pressed. I thought he was going to critique my appearance as he eyeballed me up and down for the umteenth time, but I reassessed posture and how I might stand to minimize wrinkles as I wondered how quickly I could get uniform replacements.

Then, in a quick fold and slap, he smacked the red folder down on top of others with a deliberate military-styled whack, swish, and thump.

"Who . . . *are* . . . you?" he finally asked in a measured, slow, questioning tone of voice pausing between words while frowning at me over his glasses.

"Sir?"

"Were you the colonel's driver in Nam?" He raised one eyebrow.

"No, sir." As much time spent reading my entire file, wouldn't he know that?

He exhaled a sarcastic sigh, "Is your father a governor or member of congress or something?"

"No." I must have worn a sincerely puzzled or at least innocent expression on my face. I dropped the "sir" but remained composed and polite. I was at a complete loss for what he was driving at as he continued to badger me.

"C'mon, marine. Your file doesn't tell me any details, just some odd comments and some copies of letters from people whose name I recognize."

"Okay, and?"

"I don't want to hafta read all this goddam crap," he said with a little sarcastic resignation in his voice.

"Really, Top. I don't know what you're getting at."

"Oh, really? Then tell me why in hell would the Commandant of the Marine Corps request to see *you*?" he uttered slowly with more than a touch of derision as he removed his glasses. "He doesn't talk to corporals!"

I thought he surely must frown at everyone all the time. He looked less friendly and less trusting, staring at me while tapping that pen on the desk presumably waiting for a more suitable response.

"*The* Commandant? Why . . . why, I have no idea!" Being taken completely aback, my own eyebrows arched. I felt like a little boy caught with his hand in the cookie jar. Shoulders shrugging, I felt two inches shorter; every wrinkle in my shirt was a crease upon my self-respect.

"C'mon, Choc, don't play dumb with me. Y'know right well the CMC doesn't ask to see every jarhead back from Nam. Why you? C'mon, help me out here, marine, no games! Or will I hafta call President Johnson to find out?" His half-raised, snickering smile wasn't meant to communicate humor.

"Haven't the slightest idea. Honest!" Nervous, I straightened my belt, tucked my chin, and looked down at my under-polished shoes.

"Okay, okay. You don't hafta talk to me. I'll find out. I'll just call Williams; stick around a sec." He seemed a by-the-book NCO, formal, polite, but lofty too. "He'll tell me, if you won't." Then he barely smiled to himself with a cocky, bluff-called confidence as he clicked his glasses open on top of my now-reopened file.

It was by now after four o'clock.

Of course, having no other plans to do anything else but what I was told to do anyway, I said, "Yes, sir," again, keeping good graces.

I remained standing with my hands behind my back as still and as correct as I could. I watched him raise his gray eyebrows again as he ticked through an index card file with one hand, lifting the telephone to his ear with the other. He pursed his lips. Still flicking cards, Top finally dialed a number, phone cradled on his shoulder. I surmised it must be to Williams or maybe a covert friend in a basement office somewhere.

In low, polite tones I *could* overhear, he pronounced my name in conversation, and then spelled it out "No, that's C-H-O-C."

I couldn't otherwise hear clearly what was being said at this end. I tried to eyeball the open document but couldn't get close enough to examine the paper-clipped note attached to the red file. After hanging up, Top instructed me to report *exactly* at 0915 (i.e., 9:15 AM) the next morning to the Navy Annex. I received thorough directions which he let me write down along with details about where I'd sleep that night, where the mess hall was, and where transportation would pick me up at 0800 out front of this building.

Eyeing me with tightened lips, he said, "Look sharp, marine. Most guys never *ever* get to *see the* commandant, let alone actually meet him. In twenty years, I've only seen the commandant myself close up once when I passed him in the hall! I don't usually take the elevator to that top floor."

He dismissed me dispassionately. After handing me a single sheet of orders to get me into the Navy Annex, he twisted around, set my file on the credenza, stapler on top, and retreated back into his haystack of papers as I departed.

I checked into my quarters as I was supposed to, but my piqued curiosity about why this was even happening evolved into trepidation. There was no way I could get my uniforms professionally cleaned and pressed. Since my good summer-dress shirt was a bit wrinkled, I carefully refolded it along with my good trousers and placed them under the duffel, hoping the few remaining wrinkles might flatten out overnight. Since there was no one around to ask and I didn't know my way around Arlington, I concluded this would just have to do.

For all activity around the area, these receiving barracks were oddly empty. A group of six others at the far end of the room seemed to know each other. There were maybe fifty empty bunks in these spanking-clean accommodations. I chose a bunk next to one that looked occupied at the opposite end.

As was true for all the rest of the bunks, mine was linen ready with perfect hospital folds. I'm not sure who took care of these tasks or what I was supposed to do with dirty linens. This must have been a reception or transition barracks. There were brief directions about where to go for various essentials but no other explanations from the sergeant in charge; he did issue me a sticker for my VW, and I parked it where it wouldn't get towed. I found the mess hall and ate a good meal.

The guy in the next bunk, Mike, came back in after nine o'clock in a perfectly tailored blue dress uniform. We didn't talk much, but I did find out he was from upstate Minnesota; he modestly told me about a medal he had been awarded in a ceremony that afternoon and little else; he didn't seem to want to engage in any conversation, so I obliged his privacy.

One marine at the other end switched off the lights around ten, causing chats to end. Lights in the *head*, the word for bathroom in marine lingo, remained on all night at our end of the barracks. Notwithstanding an odd day, precious sleep took minutes to capture my soul, probably more from unacclimated time zone changes and pure exhaustion.

The Trek

Immediately following 0630 reveille, I borrowed Mike's shoeshine gear, polished my dress blacks, and tidied up linens like everyone else. After showering and shaving, I repacked my duffel, setting it aside as instructed. My shirt looked better as a result of my flattening strategy, at least I believed it did, and I carefully tucked both corners tight in back to assure two perfectly vertical Marine Corps pleats as well as to stretch any lingering wrinkles yet further, cinching the web belt tight. After pleating my khaki tie tight at the neck, I looked myself over critically in the mirror. I thought I looked acceptable for customary situations even though today was definitely anything but routine. Why would the CMC want to see me of all people?

At the transportation pick up nearby, a ready marine driver anticipated my arrival. Though a corporal-like version of me, he didn't say even one word except to confirm my name, "You Corporal Choc?"

I approached the shiny olive drab, freshly washed Ford Suburban. Without further exchange, we drove the short traverse to the Navy Annex amid intense rush hour traffic and cars competing for parking places.

Navy Annex is a wide tan building, intimidating in formality and sheer size (not to mention, of course, its reputation). Everybody recognized it as capitol of the US Marine Corps. No one I knew had ever been there before.

Of course, not knowing anyone or the purpose of my mission, I became intimidated. I was becoming more and more nervous the closer I got to the entrance doors.

Walking into a spacious main lobby, a young female marine captured my eye at the first reception desk. It looked like it was her job to help people, and I needed some direction and reassurance anyhow. So I paused and engaged her in some conversation. I was taken aback by an engraved nameplate "PFC Combat Reveille" as if it were an authentic name. As I recall now, the spelling of "reveille" was different, but I know it was close. I couldn't resist wanting to ask about her name as I approached the desk.

She saw me scrutinizing the nameplate and her eyes lit up as she said, "Yes, that *is* my real name. How can I help you, marine? You look kinda lost."

I could tell she enjoyed the attention her name brought her. She grinned a quick smile that easily attracts someone almost lost or not. It's easy to cave-in to such pretty smiles, especially in the absence of typical Marine Corps sarcasm and random authority. Disclosing orders to report to the commandant, PFC Reveille pointed to the elevators, giving me explicit instructions where to go.

"You're early, y'know." She then informed me that she'd call someone to alert my arrival.

I was of course surprised by her name and decided to ask her about it. She explained, "My father's a marine officer, married to the Marine Corps, and if you can guess the rest, you'd probably be right. Actually I think he wanted a son to follow in his footsteps, but I don't think I've been disappointing him." She smile-winked. "Now, you're going to need to be patient, corporal, y'know, 'hurry up and wait' and all that stuff."

She sure knew how to make a guy feel better, and I needed that right this minute.

Toward rows of elevators, remarkably there were no other security checkpoints. I appreciated that the woman marine was both comfortable and proud of her name, but it seemed unfitting for someone as nice looking as she was. Maybe she just liked attention. I wondered what friends called her, or if she used a nickname, surely not "Commie" or "Batty." I chuckled at the play on words while pressing the "up" button. Three people made it into the elevator going up; each pushed buttons for the third or fourth floors, and I could tell they knew each other. I pressed the top floor button. I could tell it didn't go unnoticed when they eyed my finger, but nothing was said.

I distracted myself with daydreams as my stomach muscles once again trembled, unable to divert anxieties. Getting to the topmost floor, alone by this point, I exited and followed signs. Walls were lined with historical photographs; floors shined spotlessly mirror clean. People on this floor were either uniformed or in dark suits. No one talked, but just walked fast as if they were either on a mission or late.

After locating an oversized waiting area with overstuffed couches under an array of oversized photographs depicting helicopters and war ships and an unoccupied reception desk...I sat down as I could tell unconditionally this was *the* place. No one else was lingering near here. Several flags with bright golden-yellow fringes welcomed guests in this open, carpeted waiting corner with two large polished US Marine Corps brass insignias on both of the wide wooden doors. I studied the photographs and recognized hoards of Huey helicopters photographed in Vietnam settings.

Eventually, a warrant officer approached from the same way I had and asked who I was, then looked at the pass the first sergeant had given me earlier.

He said, "Hm," and then, "Stay here," in an efficient, professional manner as he purposefully marched off without further comment.

"Yes, sir." It was the only response needed, even though he left so hastily through one of the insignia-crested doors, I'm unsure he even heard it.

After coming back, he sat down and began typing, frequently making or taking very short phone calls using words I couldn't decipher. By now it was 0855 according to the twenty-four-hour Marine Corps desk clock. Being early, my promptness was for naught. A full hour passed without further dialogue or eye contact, I just presumed this was how it worked in the nation's capital. Reading magazines and further adjusting shirt wrinkles was all I could accomplish.

Pleased I didn't need to go to the bathroom, I relaxed in a purposeful way. I mused about going into the mountains back in Albuquerque and having beer drinking contests with the guys back in the day as my gut reflexes churned and I had to pee. I'd always win the contest about who could hold it the longest. I recollected what that doctor had likely done to my urinary sphincter more than fifteen years ago, and how it may have contributed to this valuable attribute.

That was then; but here, it finally became evident I had to pee. I looked around wondering if it were wise to interrupt the warrant officer from concentration and never-ending phone calls to go searching for bathrooms.

Then his phone rang again.

16

Summit Meeting

October 1967

After this particular three-second phone call, the warrant officer[1] looked my way and beckoned me to follow through the right-hand door a couple minutes after ten.

He asked me to wait in an antechamber, an internal reception area with markedly better furniture, freshly cut yellow flowers, photos of President Johnson shaking hands with generals before getting on board Air Force One, and another photo showing a group of three aircraft carriers at sea. Next to these was one oversized autumn scene of a hilly park painted in yellow, brown, and orange oils in a fancy frame that didn't seem to fit among the black and white military photos.

Becoming even more uneasy, I pondered how I should stand at attention. Making sure my piss cutter was folded appropriately under my web belt, I glanced in a mirror to make sure everything else was where it was supposed to be, and I was happy I had gotten a haircut the day before. Again tightening my shirt pleats in back, I hoped remaining wrinkles in my uniform wouldn't be noticed by anyone. My forehead was damp despite air conditioning, and I still had to pee. I decided to sit in one of the leather waiting chairs.

In about three minutes, a first lieutenant (O-2), major (O-3) and "full-bird" colonel (O-5) arrived. I stood at attention as the lieutenant said, "At ease, Corporal." Each put me further at ease with smiles and impromptu small talk about Vietnam for a minute until undetectable signals okayed us to enter *the* oversized room with overstuffed chairs, couches, bookshelves, plants, and a massive mahogany desk flanked by a row of flags.[2]

Outside windows showcased Arlington, Virginia, and silhouetted the commandant. The colonel said "General Greene?" in polite, almost reverent tones.

To my left, I could see the Washington Monument in the distance. I zeroed back in when the colonel gently repeated, "General Greene?" once more.

The general nodded while assembling stacks of papers, saying nothing as he checked his initials on a few more before sweeping them aside. Pushing his broad leather chair back an inch or two then resting one palm down over the other hand at arms-length, he looked up and (I assumed) waited for me to approach in front. His uniform was pressed flawlessly tight with colorful displays of medals in six or seven rows with his four lapel stars shining. He smiled in a grandfatherly way, obviously knowing how to create a right image promptly on cue.

I tucked my chin downward and responded to the side-whispered "orders" from the colonel. I inched toward the front of this beautiful, extraordinarily wide, hand-carved desk, as he pushed a vase of freshly cut flowers aside. I remained standing with my face looking dead straight, and then he looked right at me.

Commandant of the Marine Corps, the highest ranking officer in the US Marine Corps, finally stood and declared, "At ease, Corporal," before I could say any formal words—words I would usually say addressing my company or battalion commander. He was much shorter than I would have expected, especially for the very highest ranking marine; but, his photographic smile and warm composure made me more comfortable.

"Please, be kind enough to sit down. How was your trip across the Pacific?" he said sincerely, staring straight into my eyes as he opened one palm toward me to shake. I didn't realize shaking hands was correct protocol, but I did anyway.

"Gentlemen, please," he said directly to other officers waving toward a row of narrow but nicely upholstered armchairs whereupon he sat down and leaned back himself. There were no other formalities. Officers fell into chairs next to me one at a time like dominos.

"It was ten or eleven hours in the air, sir. I finally landed at El Toro." I could now clearly see his face and found myself staring.

"I'm happy you had a few weeks with family, Corporal." Though preoccupied with other papers, he remained attentive to my words. His voice was measured, low, yet respectful and courteous at the same time. This was obviously his throne exuding a combination of comfort and power that needed to be instantly honored, even admired. Nevertheless, he exuded a graciousness that made me at ease even though I was completely overwhelmed.

With innocent abandon, I said, "Thank you, sir." A strange pain entered my gut.

To the Point

After pleasantries and basic exchanges such as Albuquerque being my hometown, I concluded he was just making me relaxed. I noticed he had additional reference information by his right hand.

"Are you wondering why you are here?" he asked. He smiled while resting one hand over the other again, leaning back slightly. The chair made an audible, leathery crunch.

"Yes, sir, I am."

"You remember that long letter you wrote me, don't you?" he asked as he lowered his chin and raised his eyebrows to look at me over his glasses. He was barely smiling. His head tilted slightly sideways and his jaw tucked down to his khaki colored tie. His eyes met his eyebrows without uttering another word.

Blood gorged my head. Seated to my right, three stoic officers listened; one folded his hands and cleared his throat. Seconds passed with a pregnant pause heating up my face. Yes, I had written a letter to the CMC a year prior. It flooded back. I immediately tried to recall details about it, my mind reloading fast.

I responded modestly, "Yes, sir."

My face felt hotter, then chilled. My nostrils tightened and arches in my feet tingled.

I felt conspicuously stupid and vulnerable. My brain adjusted to another invisible helmet that momentarily weighed in over my ears as I maintained artificial composure during pauses that followed.

"Well, you'll be interested to know I kept that letter. It was well written, and I told your battalion commander how impressed I was with it, too. I doubt he had time to talk to you, but a formal response was unnecessary until you returned stateside anyhow."

He put both hands behind his head and relaxed further, giving me time to collect my thoughts. As he smiled his PR smile, the officers began smiling theirs on cue as well but said nothing. Everyone simultaneously leaned an inch or two back into his chair just like the four-star general had, except me.

My eyes watered, but I didn't dare wipe it away. I had to pee so badly—a pain was curly-cuing its way around my belly button.

"Yes, sir?" I acknowledged questioningly, using pauses to think back to my written words.

My mind slithered from thought to thought; surely numerous others wrote letters and certainly the CMC got a huge amount of mail, mail that undoubtedly a few sergeants or other staff read, not the *man himself*. Reassembling memories, I fumbled over mounds of now-dismissed details about that hand-typed letter I wrote aboard ship between San Diego and Honolulu fifteen months ago.

I remembered feeling frustrated with marine training and early assignments upon my transfer to A Company when deploying to Vietnam; I speculated about potentially trivializing three years of college that could have been better used by the Marine Corps. Clearly understanding its mission and using skills that might have served everyone better *had I been an officer*, I used this communication to depict how inherent talents might be of greater value. I criticized no one, and remembered writing several drafts until I felt my "pitch" and "heart" correctly presented my intentions.

Then I mailed it from the Vancouver the summer of 1966 just before arrival in Hawaii to make sure it could be delivered before heading west across the Pacific.

I was frankly not expecting agreement, but I did think I'd get a proper response. Once I arrived in Vietnam, I recalled how my company first sergeant had received a message my letter was received by CMC staff. Afterwards Top ruthlessly derided me for corresponding *directly* with the commandant without permission. Then expressing utter disappointment, he exhibited downright anger at me. My expressing an honest apology for diverting from the chain of command was insufficient contrition. As a consequence of that forceful but educational exchange, I thereupon wanted to forget the entire matter dismissing it all. I was labeled reckless. Embarrassed, I never thought about it again until this very moment.

Not imagining how my letter made such an impression then, I could not conceive I was making a very good impression this very minute either. I scrutinized self-perceived wrinkles in my shirt.

"Yes, sir, I understand and appreciate your interest. Thank you." That was all I could think to say.

I lowered my head, unconsciously avoiding eye contact. Didn't it matter that I violated the chain of command? And how many other marines wanted to become officers? How many of them wrote letters? What physically happened to all those letters others wrote; were they just thrown away? My mind was getting dizzy.

Cutting to the Choice

"Well, Corporal, has your mind changed over the last year? I mean, you still want to become a Marine Corps officer?" He had this ongoing, affectionate demeanor like he might be comfortable with a couple of grandsons sitting on his lap wanting to stay home instead of going to school.

Still holding his sculpted familial smile, his question seemed honest as his eyes lowered to his notes. "You appear to have good skills, admin school, language school, and a perfect language aptitude test score; I've never seen *that* ever before. USS Vancouver . . . um . . . now *that* was unique, of course, decent record. Hill 55, good. Khe Sanh, respectable performance reviews. Plus there are several particularly interesting side notes here and there written by men I personally know and admire." His eyes met mine again.

I wanted to give a prompt response, but I hadn't anticipated the question. "Yes, sir, I would, uh. Yes sir, I'd . . . uh . . . be *honored*. Of course, sir, I would be *truly honored*," I stammered; regaining ground, hoping he wouldn't detect my awkwardness or see that invisible helmet. I looked right at him. I paused.

Keeping posture straight as I tensed my thigh muscles, I met his eyes. "I'm sorry, sir. I guess I wasn't prepared for the question, that's all. Yes, sir, I would, absolutely."

"Tell me more, son." Grandpa General said enunciating words in subdued tones.

"Sir, I've had several particularly unique experiences. Each time I gained something of value that led to yet further unique opportunities. I'm admittedly intimidated today because I have no experience or training having conversations like these, but I do believe this to be another one of those opportunities." My peripheral sight caught the colonel's head nodding toward the general.

"Fine, corporal, let's see what we can do," he said and repositioned himself to his desk and looked at me in an authoritative, yet untypically Marine Corps, way. It was empathy uncharacteristic of high-ranking officers I had experienced up to now. He paused, thumb and index finger spreading his jowls. After squeezing his chin a few seconds, he took out a piece of 6 x 9 private, off-white military stationary displaying a red flag bearing four yellow stars on its masthead, along with his rank and name near the right margin in fairly small print.

Slowly penning today's date at the top in military format, he paused for a millisecond and wrote with a large black flathead fountain pen:

Please admit Corporal Charles W. Choc to the 45th OCS at Quantico.

Nothing more, nothing less. His penmanship was clear, almost elegant. He signed his name right below the single sentence then handed it to me.

"This should do it, corporal."

Others in the room remained motionless, smiling on cue while I stared at the message. From a drawer to his right, he pulled out a matching envelope, pushing it toward me to use. Thanking him again, I was excused with generous handshakes then escorted back through the rooms. I caught him speaking to the lieutenant who I presumed must have been an aide or military secretary.

The major who escorted me out told me he'd personally arrange transportation to Quantico at exactly 1500 (3:00 PM) that very same afternoon with the admonition, "Be sure to look sharp, marine! Be ready by 1430! The Forty-Fifth OCS actually convened yesterday and began orientation this morning!"[3]

"Yes, sir," I said. My mind entered its own tornado of thoughts, distracted only by wrinkles in my sleeves, and recurring pain in my urinary canal.

Having cinched my belt so tightly, my gut ached and belly pain became intense; but, I made it to the bathroom in time and was pleased not to see any blood in my urine from a ruptured sphincter or something.

The whole CMC-in-office episode took no more than about ten, maybe fifteen minutes.

(Endnotes)

1. Warrant officers were former enlisted marines who became officers during their career, and who ranked between the highest enlisted rank, E-9, and the lowest officer rank, O-1.

2. O-1 for second lieutenant is the lowest officer rank progressing up to O-6 reserved for a one-star general, O-7 for a two-star, O-8 for a three-star. There was only one O-9, the commandant of the Marine Corps.

3. OCS was the commonly used acronym for Officer's Candidate School and there was virtually no other function for the military base in Quantico except training new officers.

17

"Butter Bar" Bound

October 1967

At precisely 1500, I boarded a brand-new, freshly washed olive-drab Chevy Suburban and was transported to Quantico in less than two hours chauffeured by a Gunnery Sergeant (E-7). I sensed how awkward this must have been for a higher ranking, indeed much older NCO with a tired but acquiescent face to be driving a passenger of my rank (E-4), age, and tenure. He was probably used to driving officers around; he never once exceeded the speed limit nor engaged me in *any* conversation.

The ride gave me time to contemplate. There was little embraceable logic. I felt embarrassed by my substandard appearance, and how I must have appeared finally deciding to attend OCS. This was balanced by how this was a significant deviation from standard practices about such things. And, this was further counterbalanced by reemergence of my self-esteem about abilities to be more than what I was. Well, my VW got safely parked, but my duffel full of civvies was onboard with me now. So many contradictions!

So many incongruities created a sense of abandon, like jumping off a cliff without time to consider what was really down *there*.

Welcome aboard

Once through Quantico's gates, several platoons of snappy-looking officer candidates were marching in formation in khakis, other platoons in bright yellow sweat shirts with large red US Marine Corps symbols on the back, and bright-red athletic shorts, lumbering through physical exercises. The grounds were full with hundreds of officers-to-be, loaded with conspicuous high-octane resolve.

After pausing in front of a small, red brick headquarters building, Gunny left without a single word or glance beyond a gravelly low-pitched "we're here" and a readjustment of his rear view mirror. I dropped my duffel on the porch, and walked in through an open doorway presenting myself to yet another first sergeant (E-8).

The only thing I now possessed in the way of orders was this 6 x 9 document folded twice in the general's own blank envelope with that one sentence directive written in an almost calligraphic style. At the end of that single sentence, ink had already smeared a bit from handling the letter so many times. The envelope already appeared creased.

"What's this, marine?" he asked with a broad, friendly smile crinkling his forehead as he placed the unopened letter to his right side as if it might have been a note or ad or something.

"I believe those are my orders to join OCS, Top."

"Looks like some sorta invitation," he said laughing, "Y'want me to open it now?" He pointed to his right. "Y'know the Forty-Fifth already started; you're too late anyhow. In the meantime, where are the *rest* of your orders?" he said with country-style sarcasm, but he wasn't being unfriendly.

I realized that orders were usually a stack of three, four, or more 8 x 10 sheets with lists of marines' ranks and names, complete with coming-from and going-to units, dates, places, and lots of abbreviations, acronyms, plus an official signature by someone in command.

"Are y'joinin' the admin or training staff?" he asked, trying to make conversation with a nonchalant smile as he fondled the envelope a second time.

"That's all I have. Oh, I did have *other* orders directing me to report to Henderson Hall, but I gave those away when I checked in yesterday. This is it!" Since he was smiling, I was smiling too. "I think orders may be coming separately. They seemed in a hurry."

He opened the little envelope and studied the message for maybe a half minute. His language was slow with a West Virginia'ish slur.

"Ohhh key! The Forty-Fifth grouped up yestiddy. I s'pose you oughta get geared up with'em now."

He leaned back. "We'll figger out details later, *Cor'prull*. Oh, by the way, son, some quick advice. There's a dozen enlisted men like you, who joined the Forty-Fifth, and y'missed greetin's . . . 'course that's too bad, but, keep these 'orders' for now and give'em to your platoon commander at staging when y'see him in a while. I'll get back to'em tamarrah; he'll know what t'do. Here, let me write down your name and ID number, though, just in case." He put my information onto a lined tablet, tore it off the page, and started a new manila file folder with my name on it in less than a minute. "At least that's done" he sighed. He looked ready to go home for the day.

"I hope you've eaten dinner, *Cor'prull*. Once you gitcher gear, I must advise you to remove *all* markings of rank from *all* existing uniforms. I'm the last person who will *ever* address you as *cor-por-al* in your life. Is that all understood, *Cor'prull*?" Still bearing his glued-on smile, he was dead serious. He exaggerated rank words with deliberate inflection for some reason. "I'll geitcher real orders back here somehow if theyins in that bew-rockcracy can find'em up there in DC. They'll show, now git!"

It was also interesting to listen to him pronounce the word corporal two unconventional ways. It sounded deliberately uneducated, not sure why.

"I understand," I said. I hadn't eaten and was indeed hungry. I thought about my one other dress uniform, my olive green T-shirts and underwear. I presumed uniforms were reissued as part of orientation. Maybe I'd find a vending machine for candy bars.

✪ ✪ ✪

Boot Camp Déjà Vu

A gopher-type enlisted man who paid little attention (he ignored my question about candy machines) led me across the parking lot then escorted me and into a metal building where more than seventy yellow sweat-shirted, other officer candidates were stacking white T-shirts and bed linens into piles. The gopher guy took my duffel saying it'd be in the squad bay storeroom with other enlisted guys' bags.

No one else spoke to me, and there were no lines, so I waited for someone to tell me what to do. No one noticed I was even there. After lulling around for a few minutes, I eventually approached a table.

A sergeant abruptly said, "Are you here to give me a break? I'm starving."

"Uh, no. I'm checking in."

"Oh yeah? Really?" He looked me over. "Damn! Well, you do know you're late, don't you? But just give me the form, you know, your #604. You'll need to get a few things."

"I don't have a #604 form."

"Yes, you do. It's the one they gave out at orientation. Everyone got one.

"I didn't attend orientation."

"Huh?" The sergeant looked disparagingly far left

then far right; it was an obviously mocking over-gestured response. "Then, sorry buster, I can't give you any friggin' clothes! You'll just hafta go around naked." It was intended to be a funny response, but he continued in a more serious tone, "I have to account for every single one of these goddamned things. Go sit down or something, marine." He looked tired. His impoliteness was more humorously sarcastic than offending but not helpful.

He stood up and left since no one else was waiting. This sergeant acted unhappy about lots of goings on; however, at least he recognized me as a marine and not a green recruit seeking "butter bars" (marine slang for brass-colored second lieutenant rank insignia bars). But unlike other previously enlisted candidates, there were corporals' double chevron stripes still on my arms. I guess that first sergeant at check-in was not the last person to ever call me corporal.

With a mattress over one shoulder, a pillowcase of sweatshirts, shorts, and a pair of sneakers over the other, everyone except me stood up (where had all these people slept the night before?). Two in-charge marines entered, and I overheard instructions from these two drill-instructor-types to follow them through a rear door to squad bays. Everyone trying to comply, I too got up and moved closer toward the group.

One DI casually stopped me and asked what I was doing. Telling him my story, I showed him the CMC's letter while explaining why I didn't have a #604 form. Looking puzzled, he said to go ahead and he'd look into it.

"Take linens, blanket, and a mattress with you. We'll fix it up later, don't worry, someone'll fix it."

He seemed tired too. I deliberated how they might account for items I carried without a #604 form (later, I learned #604s were just for uniforms, not bed linens). I wondered about how many mattresses might be unaccounted for after training, if any; just what would one do with an extra mattresses anyhow?

I smiled at government bureaucracy and caught up with the pillowcase brigade through the back door, across another parking lot, and eventually into a squad bay of about eighty empty metal bunks with exposed springs.

18

Brown Spot

October 1967

Once in the immaculately clean squad bay, bunks were chosen, I lucked out getting a bottom bunk near several other formerly enlisted marine OCS candidates. I located my duffel bag and proceeded to make my bed, something we enlisteds already knew how to do by tucking sheets and olive-green blankets neatly into hospital folds "tight enough to bounce a quarter in the middle," according to marine mythology.

All ROTC and college grad OCS candidates fumbled with these tasks, so we enlisteds gave lessons. Meanwhile, I told my no-#604-form story between hospital folds, but didn't mention the CMC... this kept commiseration friendly amid otherwise unfamiliar anxieties, plus I didn't want to disengage myself from others in this particular way.

Having been instructed to dress in shorts, sweats, white socks, and sneakers for dinner, there was further instruction regarding how to march in formation, and other do's and don'ts. As hungry as I had become, I recognized quickly how out of place I looked gathering in the Forty-Fifth's formation for chow, a skinny khaki "exception" amid a sea of yellow and red athletes.

Each time one of the two DIs spoke to us as a group, his demeanor became more precise and stern. Each said in authoritative tones that he wanted no mistakes or inconsistencies, but neither DI paid direct attention to me. Was this on purpose or accidental? I wanted them to approach me privately to tell them my story. After all, I had no shorts, shirts, *or* sneakers!

Forming outside the squad bay, the DIs began singling out certain guys for being noncompliant with errors in feet position stance, speech, or eye contact; it was indeed boot camp all over again. Of course, it *was* boot camp, but different: more formal, cleaner, neater, higher class. We twelve former-enlisted were better prepared with fundamentals, and cited as examples to copy for the other sixty or seventy candidates.

We twelve exited the squad bay together while the rest grouped in clumps outside as the DIs tried to line us up formation, an ocean of yellow sweat-shirted participants in red shorts plus me . . . in brown. No one spoke to me. I couldn't determine if anyone was actually looking at me, but I knew I was conspicuous!

Meanwhile, my boot camp mentalities kicked back in. I was intimately familiar with formation making how-to stuff.

After some verbal orientation by an enlisted OCS candidate for about ten minutes so we could take synchronous baby steps onto the parade grounds, we marched toward chow escorted by the DIs' new second-in-charge appointee who didn't say or do much else. It worked.

Heading toward the mess hall were other sweat-shirted, more senior platoons. We stood out as rather uncoordinated—obviously newbies. Eventually it was our turn to enter. Not having had lunch, I was definitely ready to devour!

Inside, we approached the first station to pick up aluminum trays and a captain walking toward us stopped and buttonholed me.

"Why aren't you in uniform, marine?"

As appropriate to do, I stepped out of the chow line and told the story.

After I cited the #604 part, it irritated this officer, and he said gruffly, "Either you're an enlisted OCS candidate, have uniforms plus a #604 for your sweats . . . or, you're an OCS recruit and issued a #604 going through orientation yesterday. You have at least one uniform (which explains why he called me "marine"). Why aren't you wearing the correct uniform? It's not summer any longer; I think you know that! Why in the world are you still wearing your stripes, Corporal Brown Spot?" Obviously annoyed, his eyes pointed at me like crystal blue swords carving out a brown letter "B" on my chest not unlike Hawthorne's *The Scarlet Letter*.

"I was not issued a #604 upon my joining the Forty-Fifth, sir."

He said he'd make sure I got the #604 by the time I was back in squad bay. We didn't talk further about stripes.

I had difficulty recognizing anyone from my unit because I didn't really know any of them. I had to search this ocean of yellow shirts to find a familiar face in order to find a place to sit down. I finally got to gulp down fried chicken, peas, and corn. Fortunately, I took small portions, ate quickly, and "Corporal Brown Spot" meshed back into the Forty-Fifth's stream of flowing red and yellow sweats as we all streamed out the exit . . . but with me carrying a touch of fried food indigestion.

We formatted into our platoon positions neatly, lefting and righting our way in time and on time to a new building a half mile away.

Holy Chevrons!

After chow, a more comprehensive, two-hour orientation was interrupted just as it began when, at the front of the room, that very same captain pointed right at me to the OIC (officer in charge) and asked I be excused.

Now that I was going to miss second orientation, I speculated about what else I'd miss and how to make it up while this captain and I marched quickly to another building. In this warehouse, he surrendered me to a sergeant who unlocked the door grumbling about having to come back to open up just for me (this captain signed off a temporary #604 so I could get sweats and shorts). To this sergeant, it was probably a petty purpose for this late hour. Bemoaning being late for a date as he looked at me, he guessed my sizes and hastily stacked stuff on his counter without asking me anything.

The big question, however, were sneakers: size 14 narrow. After opening numerous shoeboxes and not finding *any* in my size, he eventually came around the counter to examine my feet, grunting again to confirm extreme narrowness...then said, "I've never seen such goddam narrow feet in my life! I got some wide and extra wide 13s even 14s, might get some mediums in, but you really do need narrows. Damn!" After twenty minutes of noisy fumbling around in back, he shrugged and said, "We're outta luck; I'll make sure something is here tomorrow, or maybe the next day, okay?"

He closed up shop, instructing me to go to my squad bay and change into sweats and shorts then changed his mind when he realized I'd have to wear polished black oxfords with white or black socks with my new shorts if I did that. Scratching his head, he was still obviously eager to get going, so he just shook his head and shooed me out saying he'd fix it somehow; in the meantime, "Just explain it to your platoon leader."

I went back to the squad bay with my load of new clothes as the others were filing into the room as well. By this time, it was around 2115 (9:15 PM). I wondered what that captain would think when he saw me next time.

At least, I had my sweats . . . as well as lingering indigestion.

"Lights out in twenty-six minutes," bellowed the DI. "Ex-*act*-ly! Make that twenty-*five* minutes, ex-*act*-ly!"

We made our way through one long, narrow, very public bathroom, brushed teeth, peed, and got clothes put away amid twenty-five minutes of chaos. There were more guys than basins and johns. Sharing same sinks meant bumping heads if you weren't careful how to time one's spitting.

Lights flashed once before going out five seconds later. We scrambled in darkness for correct bunks, but no one spoke. This was hard to do quietly among hushed mumbles and ouches, but DIs were silent and didn't enter. My glasses went into my shoes to avoid misplacing them. I lay face up letting toes touch the bunk railing.

I was exhausted, not sleepy.

In less than five more minutes, everyone was lying in their bunks when the DI finally did walk through, admonishing three guys for being slow. After doors slammed shut, everything became quiet. I realized rank insignias were not yet removed from my only two shirts! I waited a while to assure I wouldn't make unnecessary noise for DIs to overhear. Others were already snoring. In the dark, I opened my duffel, pulling out both dress shirts.

Light coming in through the windows allowed images to appear as my night vision adjusted. Every sound I composed with zippers and shoes were like shadowed whispers. Now the only one awake, I took a double-edged blade out of my razor and sliced sewn stitches from around each insignia. On first try, I ended up cutting holes the size of the insignia itself from both sleeves. The shirt was ruined!

More wary on the second shirt, I was careful but still tore a bit of fabric off the shirt. Not as bad as my first catastrophe, one sleeve still had a small unnoticeable cut, the other a conspicuous flap of fabric. Terrible! Frustration mixed with dread. I folded this better shirt carefully, and tried to sleep with tearing eyes wide open and wet cheeks, body sweating, ankles slick.

I finally did pass out from mental exhaustion or maybe from fright shutting down all the rest of my body's vital organs.

I awoke to blasting buzzers. The signal meant we had forty-five minutes to shower, shave, brush, and dress . . . all eighty of us! There were several red razor nicks and whiskered necks. Every soaking wet towel dripped wherever hung. Toilets flushed; two plugged ones overflowed. Faucets hissed. It was utter Clorox-smelling pandemonium with eighty half-naked guys bumping butts, swarming around foggy mirrors, and slipping on the slick concrete floor. I learned it was smarter to shave first and take showers second.

Two DIs simultaneously ordered us to break out into sweats and shorts, so I did and wore my recently polished oxfords with new white socks. After we lined up, the DI asked about my shoes in a brusque, irritated tone, but when he considered the khaki alternative, he acquiesced with a grimace, shaking his head disapprovingly. Privately, I believed he was withholding a chuckle (I saw his belly quiver), but he maintained a forced-serious frown and pressed lips.

We started physical exercises on concrete parade grounds for a half hour before going to breakfast mess. It took us longer than others because we had trouble marching the right cadence, and stopped numerous times to start over. Eventually, we got rhythm. A day of heavy labor, nonstop exercise, getting dirty, and learning to listen to less than levelheaded orders (orders designed to teach unquestioning compliance, not merely intelligent or logical response), we ended the day exhausted mentally and physically.

My shoes were scruffy and no longer black. My ankles ached. I had blisters below each ankle where hard-leather edges rubbed through the socks.

Everyone noticed me but few took the time to talk or ask questions. Those who did never seemed to listen. I told abbreviated stories maybe three or four times that day. Interest waned for Brown Spot's fairytale. I was a curious oddball, a nuisance noncompliant, maybe a limping lizard with black feet or something.

Anti-Uniformations

The second morning we went to class, khakis were dress of the day. I didn't have any so I wore my khaki-colored summer-dress shirt with tie and khaki dress slacks. In October I didn't have any olive-green winter slacks, but the shirt was similar in color, just a different, nicer material and overall appearance for dressier occasions.

We assembled into groups, heading off to breakfast with DIs giving appropriate cadence as well as snappy critique for those messing up. I saw an officer approach the DI to say something in his ear as he looked my way. We were brought to a halt. The officer placed his hands on his hips.

"You there," he said pointing to me. "Step here a minute." I did, and he went on speaking before I could salute, "Just what are you doing out of uniform? Didn't you know summer-dress was replaced by *winter*-dress Monday?"

I then saluted, "Yes, sir!" No matter how declared, it sounded sarcastic.

"Then tell me what the hell are you doing wearing a *summer* dress uniform *here* in Quantico?" He spoke with slow, measured, sure-fire bulleted words aimed right at me never moving hip-locked arms or eyes.

I repeated my story until he interrupted, raised his buoying hand, palm down, signifying not wanting to hear more, dismissing me to rejoin my group, never acknowledging the holes in my sleeves. He did speak with the DI again and marched off, avoiding backward glances. Privately I wished he would have engaged me in some conversation so I could ask questions. It didn't seem like this was being handled correctly. I didn't like being looked at the way I was. Frustration evaporated as despair lingered a little bit more after each one of these encounters. I wasn't standing as tall as I had been. Brown Spot was smudging.

Classes in US Marine Corps history depicting Chesty Puller were followed by military health and hygiene, which was followed by the principles of engagement, over these two days interspersed with generous doses of PT (physical training).

Upon entering each classroom, different officer instructors observed my noncompliance, and I re-recited my story in abbreviated versions, but sometimes with as much added detail as I could insert. Every time, the officer would acquiesce, and class would go on. I got the feeling each instructor held me personally responsible for my nonstandard appearance. Surely one of these officers would talk to senior officers to resolve the issue.

The fourth morning after the usual daybreak disorders in the heads and showers, I wore sweats and shorts again the whole morning. My shoes didn't stand out enough for anyone to stop me. By midday my blisters were bleeding, not a lot, but enough to stain through white socks on both ankles, red blotches about two inches across.

Emotionally drained, no one to talk to within this crowd, it seemed people were always *around* me, probably talking *about* me, but no one *to* me. Nothing was changing.

Coping became perplexing; psychological, not physical. I worked hard to elevate how I viewed my own unchangeable inconsistencies around those who seemed to comply so ably.

Just before lunch, we changed into khakis. This time a very tall captain was casually passing our squad bay just as we were assembling outside, and challenged my uniform.

"You look like shit, recruit; just what are you trying to prove?" He growled, then paused. "Oh yeah, so, you're the 'no-604' brown-spotted jarhead I heard about."

I saluted. "Yes, sir!"

I didn't know what else to say. Approaching me closely, the captain looked at the holes in my arms, tugged at the fabric and put two fingers into the larger hole, touching my skin. He jerked back, rotating around to confer with the DI privately; I was thereupon excused from the group and asked to wait by myself. It seemed my own DI could have been more proactive on my behalf by now; maybe he was and I didn't know it.

After being requested to return to the squad bay, I missed classes for the rest of the day. So far, I had missed so many classes, I lost track of the list I had been keeping. I now had time to clean up my dress shoes; the black polish did cover up a multitude of leather abuse, and also good therapy for the heaviness heaving in my head as well. Becoming frustrated and depressed, I felt odd not fitting in, an embarrassment to others in my platoon who seldom engaged me in conversations or any commiseration. Did I have a communicable disease? Was I fit to be an officer? Was I on probation...or contagious?

Later that afternoon I was summoned into the DI's office, and that same tall captain and another heavyset captain were there, arms folded with serious, scolding looks on their faces.

I stood at attention until the tall captain said, "At ease, marine." After being asked yet again about uniforms, he continued, "Choc, we've all heard these stories. What we want to know is why you're here. We're tired of this crap and don't want more shit from you either! Now, do I have to ask you again?" His frown was penetrating, he sat and stared. That other captain helping with the first 604 a couple of days ago wasn't present.

"Sir, I'm not sure I understand the question."

"Okay, let's start at the top. At your DI's request, in Colonel Caputo's office I couldn't find any standing orders for you. I requested action be taken, but no one in his office knew that you even existed; there's no file! Y'know, I spent over an hour in . . . *that place* to no avail. You made me feel pretty stupid, y'know that?" All three captains stared at me. "So, what's the story?"

My DI captain chimed in before I could utter a sound, but I had virtually nothing to add, "It's hard for us to create a hearing, y'see, if you don't exist. We need to do something...like officially let you stay or maybe send you back, hard to do if no one even knows you're here. I'm afraid I had to make a special date with Caputo himself. I just thought we could be better prepared."

Then the taller captain resumed while pointing to himself, "You'll be accompanying *me* first thing tomorrow to his office, and it ain't gonna be pretty, marine!" I hadn't realized this particular captain was our company commander. Somehow I had missed that introduction. I was mixing up captains' names among other things. The meeting was over.

It was as if I were under arrest or being charged.

That night I rested my head on my pillow the way I usually did, but I couldn't sleep. I wrestled with ideas about not fitting in, and how everyone it seemed had the wrong impression of me and wondered why I was interfering. Others in the squad bay were standoffish. It was obvious I was missing classes. I was not taken seriously, and I could see how my story looked like a fairytale to almost everybody.

My body armor thickened a little more; I guess I just didn't want to be different. I didn't look like they did. I didn't feel like they did. I wasn't part of the team. I didn't understand what they already knew.

I resigned to a form of personal sadness and frustrated self-pity for not being able to figure out some way to fix the problem. I felt abandoned lying awake in the bunk. Somehow, sleep recaptured my spirit as it swirled into a frenzy of dust-layered odd dreams before again awakening to that morning buzzer on day five.

19

Approaching the Bench

October 1967

Getting up that morning, I dressed in my best of two frayed shirts and a tie, happy having had the chance to polish my shoes and being excused from red and yellow-clad drill as well. The DI asked me to wait in his office.

"By coincidence," he said matter-of-factly, "we received word you can obtain your new official #604 form Tuesday. You can pick it up here first thing tomorrow before heading over. You are now authorized to draw appropriate uniforms from inventory for everything you need."

The DI scratched his head fervently and then put on his cover at an exaggerated slant as he turned and exited unceremoniously still talking (I was guessing) to me; I followed even though puzzled by this unmilitary-like behavior. Now ten feet ahead of me outside, he continued "But, as you know, our appointment is 0900 today! So, let's get a move on!" The tall company commander joined us thirty seconds later as we walked along almost in a march format with me in the middle as if I were being police-escorted.

Nobody had told me about specific appointment details at all. I'm glad I was ready, at least as prepared as I could be.

My DI captain wasn't angry, rather in "catch 22" confusion yet now on assignment. He spoke but didn't look at me saying, "Y'know, officers must purchase their own uniforms, don't you? Of course you don't. No matter, we'll process this re-issue as if you were still enlisted." He was smiling at the situation, really not interested in anything I might want to add. "Or, it'll all be deducted from your pay; they'll decide that later."

The other captain didn't say anything to me, no explanations, no "look sharp" advice. I felt like a nuisance. I was going to court without handcuffs, of course, but ushered just like a prisoner. We three approached a receptionist then a warrant officer at another desk, whereupon the DI was excused. There were always so many desks, so many filters to pass, then stand or sit and wait, so many glances assessing my presence, so many prairie-dogging eyes looking over their cubicle panels to let me know they knew exactly who I was. They knew because the stories they heard, knew because of phone calls they had to make to research what was going on.

I was now missing breakfast; nobody thought to ask me about that.

Trying to stand tall, my mind was low nonetheless. The strangest thing of all was that I didn't have any fear harm would come to me, nor frustration per se; I had already passed by all those markers. Instead, it felt more like being isolated and discouraged ...bleary-headed, over-whelmed and weak ...embarrassed, dragged along, immaterial. Natural defenses kicked in chilling reactions, letting me demur rather than become either angry or completely despondent. I had reached a point of detached contentment ...comfortably alone. Others were merely actors on stage.

Captain escorted us into an office where we sat without conversation, so I stared at a dead plant in the corner wondering if it didn't have its correct #604 form to get watered.

Eventually, yet another captain entered the little waiting room, looked at me then exchanged some whispered words with my company commander. He asked us to enter Colonel Caputo's office. The three of us went in.

There were a major, two captains, and a sergeant major (E-9) standing in line beside colonel's big desk. Colonel Caputo was in charge of all Quantico operations. I adjusted my summer *piss cutter* under my belt. All five were in full winter dress complete with medals and hash marks. No one mentioned my summer-dress, or even observed my shirt's chevron scars for that matter. Without those chevrons on my sleeve, was I a corporal, an OCS recruit, or something less than a private but still a marine?

The walls of the room were laden with photographs similar to the commandant's including one of President

Johnson. All chairs were aligned neatly in front of the Colonel's desk as he rested his hand on top of thick stack of files. Noticing my entrance he retrieved one particular file opening it flat. Everyone sat. It seemed everyone knew why we were meeting. There was an air of resignation in the room, or maybe a feeling that we all had better things to do than deal with senseless issues like mine.

Court in Session

"Good morning, Corporal Choc. I was hoping to meet under better circumstances, but it's my bet, you know why you're here. I reviewed your file, marine, not much here, not much at all! I've talked to your company commander, even someone at Henderson Hall; they don't know much either." Caputo carefully studied the now infamous single page letter handwritten by General Greene pinching his lips. "I'm not even sure about the authenticity of, uh, these orders you presented, I'll just keep this, uh, note; but, I do intend to find out, indeed this morning. Is there anything further you wish to add to this, uh, unfortunate saga?"

There was no particular anger in his voice or mannerisms, more a form of irritation coupled with restrained sarcasm. It was really by-the-book, frustrated, government-style monotone; he merely wanted us to know who was in charge, little else.

"No, sir," I said submissively. I hadn't been used to being around large numbers of ranking officers in the same room before a week ago. Now it was like being lost naked in a police station for every meal and shower. Everyone, from receptionists to clerks, appeared interested in what was going never missing the chance to look at me, but without words. Now I was facing the judge. Though pointedly alert to my stressful situation this day, I again detected an invisible helmet hanging over my ears, the same flannel-wrapped insulation experienced less than six months before.

"In case you're wondering, I'm phoning the commandant. I prearranged my call to occur at 0920, it's just past 0915. I'll inquire about your orders. Y'know they developed quite a story around here. If there's anything untoward going on, I must warn you I won't take any humiliating lightly. Do I make myself perfectly clear?" He looked at me with dagger eyes ready for the kill, but expressed the words softly. "On the other hand, if there's something we've screwed up, we'll take care of that too." He quick-glanced around at the others. "There are enough blunders to go around here." As I tried to utter my polite military response, he overrode it saying, "*Do* you understand, marine?"

"Y'y'yes, sir, I do," I stuttered just above a whisper, overlapping his icy but steady monotone.

Others in the room also nodded guardedly as if being asked the same question.

Recomposing himself, the colonel dialed, and after two transfers and holds, finally spoke, "Well good morning, sir; yes, sir, it's good to hear from you again, too." Detecting a little nervousness on his part, his voice was nevertheless solid, and generously respectful, but I knew who he was talking to. He talked about things using names they obviously both knew, and then mentioned my name. "Yes sir, he arrived at OCS about a week ago. And that's why I'm calling . . . uh . . . no, no, nothing like that, sir. Well, uh . . . yes, in fact he's in my office right now. Yes, I wanted to talk to you about that . . . sure, I can understand your interest, sir. Okay, yes, of course I can do that, just a minute."

Putting hand over the mouthpiece, he said, "He wants to talk to *you!*"

He reluctantly handed me the phone. I had no idea what correct protocol might be. Everyone was watching me. "Yes, sir, Corporal Choc speaking," I said, using my correct rank despite my sliced-open sleeves. I probably wasn't supposed to use my rank, but did anyway. No one said anything. General Greene asked certain questions about OCS, and then more personal questions about how I was doing. "Well, honestly, sir, not very well."

My voice was measured, but my outlook had drained away. Although sad and spirit bruised, I wanted to do this right.

Relating two or three sentences about cutting sleeves, conspicuousness, and embarrassment, I hoped not to belabor these points but knew I needed to explain them nonetheless. I disclosed how I missed classes. No, I didn't know how many, but a majority of them. Unable to participate in physical training properly because of shoe size, and dealing with blisters, I disclosed multiple challenges around #604 forms. Understanding, he tendered questions about letting me restart the program with the Forty-Sixth OCS the following week.

The CMC speculated how things must have fallen through the cracks as I finally entered a yet more pensive mood, talking with the only person willing to have a genuine conversation with me. He was the very same person the president of the United States talks to for military strategies of consequence throughout the world and a proactive member of the US Joint Chiefs of Staff.

Meanwhile, I also tried to observe how these words were impacting others in the room, but could detect little from solid, emotionless, unmoving faces. I was probably inadvertently criticizing one or more of them, conceivably in front of his boss. Marine Corps protocol may likely have been violated yet once again.

I didn't respond to every one of the CMC's questions, but did say, "I do understand how that sometimes happens, sir." referring to things falling through the cracks. I didn't know who in the room I could trust or what new opinions were now being formed.

"Well, what do you want to do, son? As you would probably know we have options available." The Commandant was using his kind, grandfatherly tone.

Not feeling pressed to rush into a quick, formal reply, I still recognized his time was precious. "I'm unsure this is working as originally intended, sir. I've been thinking, perhaps I should return to Arlington."

"Is that what you want to do?"

"At this point, sir, it seems like the best choice for everyone involved."

"And, you are sure, personally?"

"Yes sir. It is the right thing to do."

"Very well, Corporal Choc, I will see to it. I appreciate your participation at Quantico, as well as for your being straightforward with me."

"Yes, sir, and thank you, sir, for all your considerations on my behalf." And that was the end of the matter, another *point-of-no-return* event to stash away into my bag of what-if stories. It became calm, neutral, yet decisive.

I returned the phone to the colonel and they spoke another minute or so with him saying some "yes sirs." Colonel Caputo retreated, probably now slightly embarrassed by the situation but wisely bypassing any humiliation for my capturing the conversation with the general.

It was Monday afternoon. Though my next report date was set for Friday, I was taken privately by the tall captain to gather my belongings from the now empty squad bay. The Forty-Fifth had left the parade grounds heading for some rope climbing. I rubbed my right ring finger and wondered about how the team and I might fare if I were not able to make it up. Whose shoulders would be volunteered?

Nobody would notice Brown Spot wasn't there anymore or had ever even been there at all.

Spiffy Again

Within an hour, brand new and approved #604 in hand, the same captain took me to another building to make sure I had every uniform I needed ... every single one! Unexpectedly, I was outfitted with new dress shirts with insignias already sewn on sleeves for summer *and* winter uniforms as well as working khakis, ties, piss cutter, underwear, T-shirts, and surprisingly a brand new web belt I really didn't need. I even received two clean Band-Aids for my ankles.

While I did have to continue using my old duffel bag and my polished blacks, this replenishment ordeal took more than an hour. I felt like I had my own private tailor outfitting me; everything fit on the first try. Impressive! They still didn't have shoes my size, but for some reason I did get more socks, both black and white, and a promise for brand new size 14-A dress shoes for pickup in Arlington by Friday.

Mid-afternoon, I was driven back to Arlington by a different gunnery sergeant in another newish olive-green Suburban. Readmission was painless; that very same top sergeant checked me in, but I'm unsure he remembered me; at least he never said anything.

I had a set of written orders in hand, this time signed by Colonel Caputo. These orders were somewhat vague about what I was going to be doing, but it was clear I was reporting in to Henderson Hall. One page in length, only one name was listed on these orders, mine.

I took all my gear into the same quarters I had before, and had my choice of bunks in that virtually empty billet as well as a ready bed complete with hospital folds and a fresh pillow. Now I had a couple of days to pick up my

VW, put everything in order while two red spots on my ankles crusted into scabs.

The next day I promptly received my official orders. On Friday, I reported to an office in Roslyn, Virginia, an off-premise extension of the Navy Annex that turned out to be in a modern business office building just a couple blocks from the legendary Iwo Jima Monument.

The author next to the Iwo Jima Monument.

Colonel Biehl and Lieutenant Colonel Roque were expecting me, welcoming me onto their staff then introducing me to other officers and enlisted on the floor. Desk already readied, I spent the day organizing it, demonstrating typing skills, and learning how to create automated paper tapes for producing multiple form letters (hi-tech at the time). I fit right in.

It wasn't clemency, but I had indeed joined the Marine Corps bureaucracy. Fading into this "expected" territory this way allowed me to better manage that stress-induced invisible helmet I'd find myself wearing from time to time. I discovered it less important trying to please everyone; after all, living up to expectations of others can be an easier choice. Living up to the anticipations of self is far more worthy, and challenging . . . another mountain yet to climb.

I was now a part of a new team, and still part of the Corps of course, even though I learned how to be inconspicuously alone.

20

Relisted Enlisted

1967 – 1970

During the next twelve months, I was promoted to sergeant (E-5) most likely for my admin skills. Others liked my performance and follow-through. I made them look good. Work could be described as governmental, military-oriented, and boring bureaucratic duties. However, it was also welcomed reprieve, not stressful or frustrating. In October 1968, I requested and received early release from my full three-year stint to enter college getting out six weeks early to attend University of Maryland full-time using tuition credits under the G.I. Bill.

Establishing geography as a major, I received my B.A. in 1970. Mom and Dad flew in from New Mexico gratified about my being first on either side of the family to earn a college degree. I finally lived up to that expectation and delivered on my promise.

Still caught up in choosing a career, *teacher* sounded good for these kinds of conversations as they always had; however, by then I had started working for the state at the

Maryland-National Capital Park & Planning Commission in suburban Riverdale.

Working for MNCP&P in the house numbers and street names department was a comfortable start. I can look at local maps even to this day and pick out street names I personally selected on that job. This was a small private legacy I savor every time I explore Washington, DC area street maps.

Parallel Lines

Never discovering exactly why Quantico had been *the* destination or why I had been singled out became just a story to share.

I presume that letter to General Greene left an impression and maybe a trigger of sorts, like parallel lines, or being an unexpected standard bearer, or learning Vietnamese, or white dust, or one of those serendipitous events that occur every so often. Who could've predicted where that simple pledge three years prior between two best friends would have led?

I'm genuinely happy about my three years in the Corps, and *Semper fi* has a particular meaning for me. My military experiences were uncommon ones I wouldn't trade for anything. Yet, I'm not sure I'd ever want to repeat any one of them again either.

Looking back, it is better being worthy for something than merely being first in line, to be content with oneself rather than making only flawless decisions.

✪ ✪ ✪

Three Green Stripes

Once I took off that full-time uniform in October 1968, I went on for about six more months in the Reserves, perhaps in a vain attempt to keep image or camaraderie in hand. But it wasn't the same. In the spring of 1969, uniforms came off for the last time. I kept one dress green thereafter in my closet; it's still there decades later.

But I continue to wear the uniform no one can see.

Gaining much from amazing military adventures, I remain exceedingly proud to have served in the Marine Corps. Although I have no stories about charging the enemy or tossing grenades, it was three formative years well spent. It ushered me into adulthood in a distinctive way.

There is only one story like mine . . . mine. I probably got the long end of the stick even though I didn't become an officer. Had I, my appointment would have triggered an extension for two or more years and probably a return across the Pacific. In that situation, maybe I would've made a military career or even encountered an entirely different collection of experiences.

But things work out for the best. I believe that to be true, without reservation...the best outcome every time. I can wake up each morning anticipating much and expecting little . . . with few disappointments. When I reminisce about this developmental period, I recall internal dialogues about what really matters and how we make the decisions we do.

It's more about choices than it is about chances.

On one hand we don't want to be odd or a brown spot, but we also learn there is extraordinary value in being one-of-a-kind. When I meet others now, I seek those who are unique; this may be why I make so few friends. I guess that's just the way it is.

Looking back on the Quantico experience, I rationalize it's better to exit politely and early than be a worm trying to find value defending the decision with oneself after the fact.

Introspections

I don't mean to belittle anyone who overcomes greater hurdles than these (there are unquestionably many), nor do I trivialize the merits being a marine officer at all! But if I were to choose to do something like becoming a second lieutenant, I'd want to do so correctly, by the book, and by terms understood clearly beforehand.

I'd want to compete evenly, win fairly, or lose using established rules of the game. Had I become an officer, I'd have to live with the fact I entered Quantico with inside connections that others, perhaps more deserving than I, did not have.

I had discovered my worm.

I couldn't accept my willingness as appropriate behavior even if this bizarre caterpillar-istic adventure could have turned me into a butterfly with yellow bars on my lapels. Grace was one lesson achieved, just without wings. Had I fit in on that Quantico day, I might never have gained this message.

How I may have disappointed the commandant remains unanswered. How I took responsibility for myself did become clearer; it wasn't surrender, it was retreat. Grandmother's oft-repeated old adage, "be careful what you wish for, you might just get it" rung heavily; I'm more careful now. And, I certainly gained something when I recalled Steve's critique about it being better to be judged by the risks we took over trying never to make a mistake.

My restlessness was sated by spring 1969. This restiveness manifested itself over the years in ways that would likely never have occurred had it not been kindled by wearing that uniform for these three years. I may have walked away from khaki shirts and piss cutters and not looked back, but embracing those three years as an integral part of a maturation process was never dismissed.

I didn't know it then, but twenty-some odd weeks after getting back to the States and just after my Quantico detour, arguably one of the most significant conflicts of the war in Vietnam took place in precisely the same locale in the shadows of those two "881" mountains at Khe Sanh, the infamous Tet Offensive. Implausible losses of life and substantial human impact occurred, both physically and emotionally for the United States, the Viet Cong, and the South Vietnamese themselves. That Khe Sanh could have been to the US by 1968 what Dien Bien Phu was to the French in 1954 made this outpost strategically crucial and historically significant after all.

Such hearts clad with tattoos, stored private, personal, permanently inked stories not easily shared despite today's cordialities, smiles, and good conversation. My path continued to cross others' paths who revealed their own inked stories, and I went on to discover how a listening ear gained another's willing confession in the same affection as one of those blood brother handshakes, even if it were just for a day, only once, or over a drink.

Most of us had learned the true meaning of the word "camouflage" and wore it well.

21

Invisibly Uniformed

1969 – Present

It didn't take long for Marine Corps khakis to evolve into Dockers' khakis once I graduated from college. Light blue button-down collar shirts with nice ties and casual 14-A shoes created the in-office image just like khaki shirts and web belts had in the marines. How one dressed in civilian life still described rank but without bars or stripes. Eventually I needed a second sports coat so it didn't look like I had only one, then a suit, then a second suit as career advanced with changes in physical locale. Those willing to move gained an edge over those who just wanted to take their boss's place; I was better at moving than waiting.

Recalling General Greene's stationery, eventually my own name was inscribed on business cards and then later stationery itself. My signature was distinctive. My rank and responsibilities expanded during the next four decades, just without chevrons. I fit the mold using rules in place finally becoming an officer after all, maybe without a military uniform but with my invisible Marine Corps chevrons on my sleeves nonetheless.

I sought less popular but personally rewarding assignments eventually allowing me to become *the* big fish in little ponds with suitable scripts to play. I had just enough limelight, recognition, and a great deal of self-determination . . . the kind of officer I wanted to be.

Life Roles

At the onset, objectives moved from military to business. Although extroverted and socially proficient at work, my natural C-plus-iosis invaded living. I was neither very social nor expansive about seizing social opportunities.

It wasn't until I was twenty-nine I married. And then, it was only to a person who might understand a narrow focus on roads less traveled. What first attracted me to Carol was her modest but un-daunting courage when she volunteered for the Red Cross and served a year in Vietnam. This coupled with genuine kindness exhibited to others created such a beautiful soul. I've met a few women in my life who went to Vietnam. Nearly all of them were overtly conspicuous to others about their sacrifice which often made them brash with their badges and accomplishments. Not so for Carol! Privately a kind person and proud of her experiences, she was indeed gratified by her own Vietnam sojourn. But notwithstanding her own achievements, few people ever came to know Carol served in Southeast Asia at all; for those who did, I was probably the one who told them.

I became similarly proud of our three sons Brian, Jared, and Tyler. I couldn't believe how completely unalike they were to each other growing up and how further unique they have become as adults.

Now there is a further generation of three boys and two girls to follow, and I am amazed to witness how their personalities are forming...how they're exercising undeveloped wings and to listen to their thoughts about where they intend to fly.

The Marine Corps was a huge fork in the road in 1965, but I had no idea how those three and a half years would impact countless subsequent decisions and shape many of my own values and attitudes. My grandmother's never-decide-not-to-decide advice was accurate.

It was forty years after discharge with decades of zig-zagging profit and loss charts, but less than completely satisfying employment that my 1960s chevron-sleeved experiences resurfaced in several odd ways.

No, there were no military uniforms. It wasn't war, but there were different kinds of trenches and tattered tents this time. Of course, I had talked to many Vietnam vets over the years, and there were all those do-you-remember-when chats. But, most chose not to share their inner wounds, dismissed them, or were not seeking out anyone to listen to fragile memories.

No, it was not my peers. Instead there was a new crop of youth about to make, or having just made, significant life decisions. I met several guys who remained sleeping in their own metaphorical bunks only to wake and wade through their own mists, alone or even choking on their own version of ethereal dust. And, I could relate.

Margaret Stuart

In Spring 2009 (I was living in Helena, Montana, at the time), I volunteered at a place called Margaret Stuart Youth Home and Shelter for male youth aged fifteen to eighteen from abusive homes situations, trivial drug-related issues, or those who might go to JDC (Juvenile Detention Center) for petty crime. Although comings and goings were monitored, if one wanted to run away, he could; some did. When caught, quasi-freedoms were traded for more jail-like environments at JDC. It was a well-kept, otherwise well-used home housing eight youth at a time where I hung out for two and a half years.

The residents fought for either supremacy or privacy while always managing to challenge staff. They had to figure out how to fit in, and each seemed hungry for both calories and rank. Being polite, tidy, or well-groomed were attributes none sought nor exhibited. However, they did have strength in body, character, or street-logic. Many had been physically abused usually by dominant fathers. Just like so many Vietnam war veterans, body scars lay open as telltale evidence of battles fought, yet emotional scars were shrewdly disguised and seldom ever shared.

After passing the can-he-be-trusted tests that streetwise teenagers manufacture, and though I wasn't a state-appointed psychologist, or wearing a badge, or toting a bible, I was accepted into *their* household with a teenager's graciousness few adults could earn, let alone recognize or appreciate.

After staff's respect was garnered, I was availed privileges just short of being a staff person myself. I was a marine, Vietnam vet, but I didn't throw myself around as just another authority figure. These things made me interesting despite my white hair.

Typical initial encounters involved talking about interactions, games, or helping with homework. This evolved into once or twice a week coffee outings. While drugs were off limits, caffeine was the closest legally usable drug, so it was attractive in that sense; plus it was adult-like, therefore a sought privilege. I'd listen attentively to what was bothering them, ask about ongoing issues, and never duck a question no matter how intense, probing, or irregular.

Snipes and Crime

Regaining trust for older males was a tough road for resident youth, and I learned from staff (and in separate training forums) these behaviors tended to repeat into the next generation if not reversed. I think these young men were unconsciously hoping for good adult models to copy.

It was appalling to learn how often illicit drugs were introduced to these boys by parents in the same way after dinner drinks might be offered to adult guests visiting their homes. My reactions were camouflaged to avoid appearing judgmental. After all, their home settings were viewed as normal by them, and they were merely copying parents' conduct. I never judged a young man's family or upbringing.

Off grounds, nearly everyone smoked. This was unpermitted at Margaret Stuart since nicotine was illegal for minors. It was more important for me to ignore this bridge drug to gain respect, appreciated by residents and privately tolerated by staff who knew these goings-on occurred off premise. Nicotine while unhealthy was significantly less dangerous or punishable than ill-chosen behaviors already on their biographies. If nicotine addicted, withdrawal stress would be counterproductive on many levels anyhow.

The residents earned small allowances doing chores with positive attitudes, but they still had little money to buy much. Because they were unable to buy cigarettes legally, they either found stores where they could or other ways to do so, taking pride finding places to hide small inventories of contraband. Sometimes staff discovered stashes and penalties were given out; too many penalties and the teen would lose his privilege to leave the building unaccompanied by staff who would not tolerate *any* aberrant behavior. When addicted to nicotine, it produced withdrawal anxieties coupled with immature decision-making, which inevitably led to relocation to JDC if not well managed. When this occurred it was repeatedly used as *the* example to deter witnesses from copying similar behaviors; it worked at least for a while.

This is why several teenagers liked to go "snipe hunting" as an additional task after our mutual coffee sojourns. *Snipe* was street lingo for a cigarette butt discarded by others;

typically two or three more good drags could be reclaimed. Snipe tobacco could also be rerolled into a longer five or six hit cig. Hoards of snipes were carefully hidden off grounds near Margaret or inside coat linings or pant cuffs. It was a game, a challenge, a worthy goal to pursue in their eyes.

Respects and Rules

Dealing with authority was the biggest issue. Since Margaret had rules, a common challenge was testing limits and gray areas of interpretation for every single rule. Residents studied rules tangibly and publicly, quick to point out inconsistencies with some success half the time... sponsoring further explorations into the ever-entertaining talents of rule breaking. These young men weren't dumb! I witnessed confrontations between staff and residents, often displaying intelligent belligerence occasionally requiring physical restraint. Staff was carefully trained in such matters; events were settled fast.

However, when incidents deteriorated into unacceptable territory, police were summoned with JDC as the next destination. Every six weeks or so, this had to be reproved for rookies to witness. Although these were low-paying positions not requiring high-levels of education, all staff had a fortunate strain of empathy dealing with "below the bar" youths assigned to Margaret Stuart.

Despite these givens, the service I brought to this untidy table was safe commiseration on an adult level from undereducated almost-adults. I was remarkably successful at asking questions in a Socratic-type approach, inducing the young man to come to his own conclusions; after all was said and done, he taught himself. I declined answering their what-would-you-do questions in this way hoping to bolster problem-solving skills and self-esteem.

Preaching golden rule adages had low mileage in these contexts; they even stole from each other! But the golden rule was personified by staff to reinforce reciprocal conduct. A slow process, I watched how it developed in practice over boys' tenures as this quid pro quo behavior was fortified repetitively, becoming fertile ground for each to self-invest.

Embracing parallel concepts into my own interactions with stories about how marines learned to take care of each other in life and death situations, it's important to point out I did this only when asked about these experiences; I did not preach. I underscored the value of promises kept among military brothers to stress peer respect and to assure an absence of any sort of pretentious limelight-seeking drama on my part. I gained eye salutes for this.

While there were few thank-you's, their persistent desire to go for coffee with me and probe deeper into what others thought about their personal issues was gratifying to me. When they said, "No one has ever listened to my side of the story as you have," I knew I was on the right track. That this came from a street-smart, tattooed, previously dismissed teenager doubled the value to me personally since I recognized the sincerity of these acts of appreciation, something few folks were honestly able to do.

Once in 2010, halfway through my three-month teaching English stint in Ecuador (a completely separate volunteer project of mine), I placed a long-distance call to Margaret Stuart, having a one to two minute chat with everyone present including staff. Five weeks later, I was humbled to learn from house manager, Zoe, how a line in front of the office had formed that day with each resident waiting to get their own sixty seconds of hello to someone ten thousand miles away. Cameron and Jacob told me I'd been missed. Michael said he desperately needed some marine-made coffee!

Back home, every day I would receive a Marine Corps salute when I arrived at Margaret from Jeremy. Then there were Brandon's or Kyle's handshakes that lingered more than the usual two to four seconds . . . lasting grasps coupled with an eye lock that communicated something deeper.

These "thank-you's" went beyond what might ever be anticipated. Had there been nothing else, these would have made it worthwhile, like a farmer who plants a little bag of seeds and later views a field of ready-to-harvest crops.

PTSD, TBI, and Schizophrenia

Once youth home experiences began, my "parallel lines" suggested I check in with Veteran Affairs at Fort Harrison, Montana, in 2009 to work with returning vets from Iraq and Afghanistan. Returning veterans frequently suffered from PTSD (post-traumatic stress disorder) or TBI (traumatic brain injury); both conditions provoke inabilities to easily reenter the society they left before deployment. Readjustments into social norms were encumbered by recurring stressful mental replays of traumatic events causing various forms of distancing from anything that might re-trigger that anxiety. Therapies were painstakingly tedious, full recoveries slow. Often, withdrawal and solitude were the only remedies to self-heal.

But such distancing isn't effective therapy. The brain needs different forms of positive mental exercise to reinstate common social traits . . . behaviors that were mentally broken or lost by battle trauma. The exercise vets need may seem one-sided since his spouse, family and friends treated him like they always had; but he could not reciprocate. The physical brain mends, reconnecting severed or damaged thinking patterns. I'm told synapses inside vets' brains have become impaired or broken, but they can heal themselves, albeit slowly, and only with thoughtful and gentle understanding of the process by those who know him, a painstaking process often abandoned by those closest to him.

Since veterans' understanding of this process is so uncommon, small advances in social skills only come with practice and toleration of his odd but not abnormal behavior observed by those closest physically. Their impatient partners, employers, friends, and spouses often don't recognize the context even after copious benefit-of-the-doubt acts of forgiving. This is why vets so often choose solitude.

Another hurdle vets jump is the suck-it-up attitude military service instills. In particular, I found those from the West are taught not to complain about personal vulnerabilities. Instead, just "suck it up!" Those vets are often ones least able to appreciate any small self-improvements since he chooses not to disclose shortcomings in the first place even when he looks and acts completely "normal."

This reminded me of my own plights back in 1967. Acronyms like TBI or PTSD weren't used back in the '60s, and I wasn't diagnosed with any disorder either. After becoming more formally educated on these symptoms, there is some conjecture I may have faced a form of "explosion induced stimulation" (colloquially, "shell shock"). Years after my own return, I speculated that I probably endured a form of PTSD myself after sleeping through that dusty mortar barrage; but, maybe not.

I joined Fort Harrison's VA board of directors to oversee returning military events and programs. The official intentions were valuable but more oriented toward a vet's family than the vet himself, dealing with recognition, cemeteries, chapels, and speaking events.

I also attended VA educational seminars dealing with typical psychological challenges but not so much with solutions. As a program offshoot, I volunteered to work directly with veterans. For as many vets as there were, it seemed they fell into two camps: those who were so badly wounded mentally (and physically) and needed hospitalization and constant professional care, and those who just "sucked it up" and remained anonymously at home or on the streets homeless and therefore unknown to the VA.

Over time, I discovered bars full of such military guys with nowhere to go. Still, I was able to connect with a few for one-on-one conversations. While I was easily able to relate to their overseas stories and new hurdles at home, it was hard for them to get past the embarrassment they seemed to suffer. For an investment of time and effort, my own education was augmented considerably, but I don't believe I had significant impact on the Montana program nor very many vets themselves.

Spending Resources

I tried to avoid being either pedantic or altruistic. Once I uncovered what value my empathetic attention meant to those telling their stories, it added to my own self-esteem and created a one-of-a-kind bond. The art of using such assets advantageously has been a worthy voyage unto itself. Maybe I'm proving the old adage *all I really have is what I'm willing to give away*. Harvested crops are much more than that initial packs of seeds.

In Old Bisbee, once when walking the street downtown, I bumped into a vet I had met more than a year before, a guy who probably suffered from PTSD but sucked it up. He had been playing guitar pensively at a downtown bar the spring of 2010; and, afterward over a beer, Keith and I engaged in conversation about music lyrics. After a few Socratic-type probes regarding how some military issues had affected his personal life, it evolved into matters on his mind. As a snowbird I came to Bisbee, Arizona, once or twice a year and seldom downtown by myself, so it seemed a one-time bar chat. I recall listening and asking pointed questions, perhaps questions he wanted me or *needed* me to ask.

This time (now Fall 2011), heartily surprised, he stopped me on the street and asked if he could buy me a drink right then and there. He seized this impromptu as-luck-would-have-it opportunity to tell me how consequential that prior year's conversation had been.

"You have no idea how low I was that night, amigo," Keith said genuinely.

"I do remember how emotional the lyrics sounded inside your voice," I agreed.

"No, those words *were* my heart bleeding." He explained how his fiancée of two years finally did decide to leave him and how he hit rock bottom. Nothing he could say or do seemed to matter to her anymore. "You're the only one to pick up on lyrics I had written *just* for her. She couldn't. It was a plea to nowhere. She's moved on now. That's for the best."

"Where'd she go?"

"Phoenix I think. But now I've met someone who knows how to listen to me play . . . appreciates lyrics for what they are. Her name's in songs I sing these days. I don't need much else right now 'cept to say that we're getting married soon."

Yet as he spoke these words, I felt gratified for this off-chance meeting. That 2010 chat about life issues, which I can now only vaguely recollect, turned out to be significant perhaps because I invested interest into understanding but offered no specific advice. I just made observations and asked probing questions. His recognition of those few things I said were mere seeds planted in ready furrows. Yet I ask myself today, who harvested more, he or me? How does one measure how much more one reaps over another?

I let him pay for the beers.

And so it goes.

No, I don't play bridge, tennis, golf, or garden, nor do I associate well with others my own age doing what we're *supposed* to be doing, behaving like seniors apparently do. This road I'm on doesn't have much traffic, but when I do connect, there are meaningful transactions that make it meaningful. It may be a narrow path, but it's contentment and mine to savor.

So many furrows seeded. So many fields weeded.

Recollecting this Uniformed Sojourn with Today's Eyes

What is serendipitous for some is abandoned by others.

I never fired any of my weapons at anyone in Vietnam, nor did I ever actually face a live Viet Cong soldier, though I did see quite a few dead Charlies along the way. While I did go on quite a few "rice-paddy patrols" with Captain Velasquez, I really didn't see any direct face-to-face altercations at all. Many of those who did face their enemy, probably remembered their faces.

Khe Sanh was unquestionably a tedious, boring place at times, but it was a dirty, dizzying, nasty, schizophrenic, razor-edge, dangerous place as well. Snaps or pops made you jump. The unpredictability and edginess around Khe Sanh affected certain marines more than others. Witnessing discomfort combined with fear turn into paranoia, I observed from nearby bunks how some marines physically wrestled with nightmares, stayed awake praying, writhed in their night sweats, or cried privately. Few openly admitted it or they collectively dismissed such things. Consolation was a tough commodity to find or share. For me, like an invisible flak jacket, I relied on pensive isolation, a place no one was ever invited in...a place I'm unsure was ever detected.

For other vets willing to share their feelings, my ear has offered some solace over the years since my own return because I have seen what they have seen coupled with a knack for asking pervading questions. The unintended consequence of PTSD or TBI from war is hard to reverse.

In any case, mental scars traveled home with thousands of marines. For most of us, reconciliation never materialized completely. Personally, I never did understand the justice of it all or how my journey might have been different; but, I have wondered since whether the passage had been something that deprived me of recognizing other beautiful things of possibly greater value. Or, perhaps it was the armor I'd need in order to be grateful later.

I departed Southeast Asia a great deal more than a year older than when I arrived just one year before. I learned to recognize and decipher how the facial handwriting around others' eyes matured during those years. Yes, the eyes disclosed much of the story, but twists of lips or wrinkles in the brow revealed other things. It's indeed a special language.

Compelling experiences we bring back can haunt us, like images and sounds of choppers coming in then flying out, hovering and dropping fresh troops off then hauling shiny green bags back along with the arriving and outgoing mail. There's the rat-a-tat-tat machine gun fire and unforgettable pendulums of canon fire. For so many of us, behind today's wrinkles lay some lingering unanswered questions, etched from deep inside yesterday's events.

Even when we choose not to remember, we're reminded.

In my case, perhaps I had *just enough* distancing to carry a psyche away to thrive in another world yet to come. I admit I wasn't completely immune after all. No matter how many marines or soldiers or corpsmen there were around you...no matter who was there to protect you...no matter how thick the planes or choppers were in the sky, sometimes in the end you were indeed alone.

And we then learn to reconcile.

How can anyone grasp, let alone appreciate, the weight knowing how others did what they were supposed to do then were wounded or died . . . alongside my own knowledge about what I had not done right and survived unscathed?

History has painted a wide mural of consequences on that wall map of the world for this lonely niche in the upper left hand corner of a skinny Southeast Asian country. I was at least a part of it, not the most difficult part mind you, but a role I could handle. My time was what it was. I gained tremendously from truly unique experiences and survived to traverse quite a few more stories yet to come.

I played the role handed to me with pride and insight, but there are so many others who have experiences of greater intensity and consequence ... stories that never will be told.

But among those of us still carrying these memories, we also carry one tattoo in particular ... that special boot camp lesson about how to put another's boots on our own shoulders. It's about team ... about others who rely upon us to give them that push up the rope when their own arms don't respond ... without being asked. No fingerprint on my right ring finger remains testament, reminder, my private tattoo.

Endurance and Evolution

There's a message attributed to Darwin, suggesting survival of a species is not dependent upon how many, how big, how strong, or even how intelligent that species may be. Rather, survival completely depends upon that species' ability to adapt. Whether it's a young wimpy man trying to fit into life for the first time, or working at refitting back in after extraordinary circumstances, it's all about how we manage change...how we amend our outlooks over time...and those few bedrock principles sustaining our bodies...our souls.

Over time, most of the poignant impacts of war's debris healed at home, and I discovered an encouraging after-effect many other veterans brought home with them too. I recognized how *adapting* could become a tangible human attribute to acquire. Those who could not, did not; they either died of wounds to the body or lived with wounds to the soul.

A Uniformed Dénouement

As I now reminisce, speaking Vietnamese turned out to be of no value. I watched Darwin's practical hands at work with my rusty shotgun being replaced by an M-14 then changed into a plastic M-16, but I never tested or substantiated any of these weapons' intended purpose. Dreamy images of undulating layers of dust played its own role. My particular muddy 14A footprints on the red clay of Khe Sanh were probably immaterial.

But beyond reaping Darwin's survival message, this improbable marine did earn contentment plus recognition of assets he didn't realize he had. Did he witness justice or mercy? Or was it just a series of serendipitous events?

Right now in life after all has been considered, I say the map was good, those less-traveled roads well-groomed, and the journey worthy. It may be why my old friend Puff from that favorite song continues to linger around in a tucked-away corner of my mind dubbed Honalee. After all, dragons do live forever, but not so, little boys.

Epilogue

On these roads less traveled, I recall a kids' movie, *Neverending Story*, where the ethereal cloud envelopes virtually everything at unrelending, increasing speed from all directions. You know, that "nothingness" that replaces the somethingnesses we all recognize as eternal.

Life seems to be like that.

So I write down these few more words before they get captured on that nothingness cliff of time.

Maybe it's what matters.

About the Author

Wes Choc grew up in Albuquerque, New Mexico, living there until 1965 when he joined the Marine Corps during the Vietnam era. Since the end of his military service in 1969, he worked for the American Automobile Association for over forty years. In 1992 he was appointed president and CEO of AAA MountainWest, overseeing business and club operations in Montana, Wyoming, and Alaska. After retiring from AAA in 2008, he and his wife, Carol, moved to Arizona.

Wes has become an active community volunteer. With his TEFL certificate in hand, he spent three months teaching English as a second language in Ecuador. Back at home, Wes tutors English regularly for new US residents. He also mentors homeless and troubled youth.

Wes has worked with veterans in Montana and Arizona, especially with vets returning from overseas with PTSD or other disabilities. Wes is currently an active volunteer at the Tucson Veterans' Hospital helping recovering vets. Carol and Wes Choc make their home in Tucson, Arizona.

Wes enjoys writing and has recently established his own publishing platform aptly named Chosen Journey Media. Ironically, "Just Dust – An Improbable Marine's Story" has become the first, next step of Wes' new path of chosen journeys. Wes recently went back to work and is delighted to have completed **"Inconspicuous"**, a life story told to him by a friend who also served the United States proudly in uniform.

Learn more at
www.weschoc.com

www.ingramcontent.com/pod-product-compliance
Lightning Source LLC
Chambersburg PA
CBHW050532300426
44113CB00012B/2062